Library of
Davidson College

VOID

THE INDUSTRIAL REVOLUTION
IN THE SOUTH

THE INDUSTRIAL REVOLUTION IN THE SOUTH

BY
BROADUS MITCHELL

AND
GEORGE SINCLAIR MITCHELL

AMS PRESS
NEW YORK

Reprinted from the edition of 1930, Baltimore
First AMS EDITION published 1969
Manufactured in the United States of America

Library of Congress Catalog Card Number: 75-100818
SBN: 404-00201-3

AMS PRESS, INC.
New York, N.Y. 10003

To
S. H. M.
*who joins New England
and the South*

ACKNOWLEDGMENT

For permission to use these papers in the present volume, the authors are indebted to the courtesy of the editors of the following publications: Harvard Business Review (No. 1), Virginia Quarterly Review (Nos. 2, 4 and 8), Yale Review and the Director of the Yale Press (No. 3), South Atlantic Quarterly (Nos. 5 and 6), American Labor Legislation Review (No. 7), The Commonweal (Nos. 9, 10 and 11), Baltimore Evening Sun (Nos. 12, 25 and 26), The Survey (Nos. 13 and 20), Manchester Guardian (Nos. 14 and 18), Cotton Factory Times, Ashton-under-Lyne (Nos. 15 and 17), Raleigh (N. C.) Union Herald (No. 16), Catholic Charities Review (No. 19), Manufacturers Record (No. 21), Cotton (Atlanta, Ga.) (No. 22), Religious Education (No. 23), and The Industrial South (proceedings Southeastern Economics Conference, Atlanta, Ga., 1928) (No. 24).

INTRODUCTORY

The South has run the gamut of social experience—colonization; national leadership; staple agriculture, slavery, and secession; civil war and destruction; political humiliation; and last the shift toward manufactures. Industry is not only setting past errors right, but it is determining Southern culture for the present and future. It brings perplexities, but it destroys separatism, and invites and forces national and world consciousness. No one can calculate what the South will some day be like without grasping the tremendous implication of the factory.

The papers here brought together, dealing mainly with the social effects of the Southern cotton manufacture, were written over the period of a decade. In this time the Southern industry has developed from sectional to undisputedly national significance. The decade has witnessed not only the expansion of indigenous mills, but the southward migration of Northern factories, and the movement continues unabated.

The story repeats old experience in the rise of industry. There have generally been three stages of progress. At first attention was absorbed in technical problems—capital accumulation, managerial training, growing efficiency of mechanical production, expansion of markets. Second has come the recoil of workers against exploitation—marked by extension of welfare programs, proposals for protective legislation, and labor unionism. The third phase introduces industrial maturity—establishment of a certain balance of power between human and mechanical forces, and the appearance of new problems of management, involving the stabilization of industry.

The Southern cotton manufacture, for most of the period under review, has been in the second of these stages, but now its entrance upon the third may not be remote. These years have been under a paradox—the depression in the industry following the postwar lapse of 1920-21, accompanied, nonetheless, by striking augmentation of the number of spindles and looms locating in the South. Cross-currents have made an eddy. Depression has prompted and at the same time stilled labor unrest, and the southward drift of mills has had a similar effect, for the excitement of physical accomplishment has distracted attention from human problems, while at the same time added demand for workers has put them in a stronger position.

Added to all, the Southern cotton mills have been in the spot-light of national observation. At first the jeopardy and then the draining of textile New England has focussed eyes upon two main occurrences affecting ability to exploit the South industrially. These have been the proposed child labor amendment to the Constitution, and, in the last year and a half, a series of strikes in Southern mills resulting in a Southwide organizing campaign backed by the American Federation of Labor.

The following papers punctuate this progress. In each case, the date of publication is given in the footnote. Little attempt has been made at revision, and consequently there is overlapping and, now and again, inconsistency in judgment. They have been grouped topically rather than chronologically. If the reader feels that the authors have sung the same song throughout, they accept the indictment, with, however, the explanation that they have not found occasion to alter their essential analysis, and that they have regarded themselves not only as students, but as advocates.

B. M.
G. S. M.

BALTIMORE,
June 17, 1930.

CONTENTS

		PAGE
INTRODUCTORY		ix
I. THE PROBLEM		1
1.	THE PRESENT SITUATION IN THE SOUTHERN TEXTILE INDUSTRY	1
2.	FLESHPOTS IN THE SOUTH	26
3.	SOUTHERN SPINDLES	47
4.	SOME SOUTHERN INDUSTRIALISTS	64
5.	THREE SOUTHERNERS	80
6.	TWO INDUSTRIAL REVOLUTIONS	89
7.	THE IMPACT OF INDUSTRY IN THE SOUTH	113
8.	WHY CHEAP LABOR DOWN SOUTH	130
II. RECENT LABOR UNREST		146
9.	A NEW VOICE IN THE SOUTH	146
10.	FROWNING AT THE SOUTH	154
11.	TAKING A STAND IN DIXIE	165
12.	HAYMARKET AND GASTONIA	173
13.	THE COTTON MILLS AGAIN	178
14.	A WAVE OF STRIKES	187
15.	BLUNDERING ALONG IN THE SOUTH	191
16.	STEPS IN UNION PROGRESS	196
17.	AMERICAN TEXTILE UNIONS, PAST AND PRESENT	200
18.	IN THE SOUTHERN COTTON MILLS	207
19.	STRIKES DOWN SOUTH	210

		PAGE
III.	CHILD LABOR	217
	20. THE END OF CHILD LABOR........	217
	21. THE SOUTH AND THE AMENDMENT..	232
IV.	WELFARE WORK	238
	22. COTTON MILLS IN SOUTHERN CIVILIZATION	238
V.	THE OLD SOUTH AND THE NEW...........	271
	23. THE ECONOMIST LOOKS AT RELIGION.	271
	24. ANALYZING OURSELVES IN THE SOUTH	276
	25. SLIPPERS AND OLD SORREL........	280
	26. SAND-HILLERS NORTH AND SOUTH..	287
	27. SOCIAL EDUCATION	292

THE INDUSTRIAL REVOLUTION IN THE SOUTH

I. THE PROBLEM

1. THE PRESENT SITUATION IN THE SOUTHERN TEXTILE INDUSTRY [1]

Some would have it that the industrial South is being born. I prefer to present it as in adolescence. Industry in this section had its inception in the 'eighties and 'nineties, flourished through a quick youth, and is now in the difficult years preceding maturity. It possesses important inherited characteristics and it may have certain " fœtal memories " that help to explain its present disturbed state. But, by and large, vexatious behavior did not make its appearance until recently, after the depression which followed the Armistice.

I have tried elsewhere to trace the beginnings of industry in the South after the Reconstruction period. This turned out to be a straightforward story of progress at a gratifying pace. There were elements, to be sure, which one labeled as requiring adjudication some day—child labor, long hours, the extreme paternalism of the company-owned mill village, the deafness of Southern legislatures to the call for restrictive regulation. But the need of the

[1] April, 1930.

impoverished South was for opportunity to work, and the benison of creativeness was poured over all.

For a period the cotton-manufacturing industries in the North and the South (we may neglect the rest of the country) developed prosperously side by side; they were, however, more or less distinct in products, markets and labor management. But now that the slack in the rope is being taken up, and margins of profit have dwindled or disappeared, perplexities and conflicts arise. These apply both within the South, and as between North and South. Progress of the cotton-mill South has brought it to the van of the marching column, where it must catch step with the North and, indeed, with the rest of the textile world, or there will be confusion out of which a new tactic must be evolved. The eyes of the country are now on the South because of the 15 strikes, three of them of major proportions, which have occurred there in the last 10 months. There have been the usual accompaniments of violent industrial difference—picket lines, denial of civil liberties, calling out of troops, evictions, floggings, killings, trials, sentences, exaggerated abuse on both sides. But in the suddenness of the flare-up, the speed with which the flame spread to new places, the eagerness to berate the South from without and the evident astonishment within it, even the casual observer is persuaded of novelty.

First of all, the South has scarcely begun to realize what is happening to it economically. The pace of its industrial advance, particularly in the cotton manufacture, has been breath-snatching. Between 1925 and 1927, the latest years for which there are government census figures, the cotton-growing States increased the number of their cotton mills from 809 to 834; they had in 1927 almost 62 per cent of the total number of establishments in the country. The number of wage earners in these two years increased from 246,974 to 281,390, or from 55.5 per cent to 60.2 per cent of the country's total. The value of their products declined from $929,107,000 to $900,627,000, but the value declined more in the rest of the country, so that the percentage of the value belonging to the cotton-growing States increased in two years from 54.2 per cent to 57.5 per cent. These gains were mostly at the expense of New England, which lost 30 establishments and 9312 wage earners, and declined in value of product from $607,925,000 to $519,219,000, or from 35.5 per cent to 33.1 per cent of the country's total.

North Carolina, the leading cotton-manufacturing State in the South, long ago passed Massachusetts, the leading State in the North, in number of establishments, and now has far more than twice as many individual mills; but it was only recently, between 1925 and 1927, that Massachusetts lost supremacy to North Carolina in number of wage earners and in value of products: Massachusetts dropped from 96,182 workers to 90,875, while North Carolina mounted from 84,139 to 95,786; and while the value of products of Massachusetts fell from 20.2 per cent to 18.2 per cent of the total of the country, those of North Carolina advanced from 18.4 per cent to 19.8 per cent.

In the face of all this, the South's fundamental reaction is surprise, and closely linked with this are resentfulness of criticism and pleasure at the new-found material sufficiency. Mr. Paul Blanshard has said aptly that the South at this juncture is laboring under " the elation and obfuscation of the victory mind." The whole attitude of the section reaches back to the agricultural South of slavery, the fighting South of the Civil War, and the punished South of Reconstruction.

Agriculture meant a static economic tradition. From the introduction of the cotton gin until 1880 the South admitted, broadly speaking, no new forms of economic effort. The early part of this period witnessed the gradual decay of small and varied manufactures, followed not long afterwards by disappearance of the last organized protests against Negro slavery. In the late 'forties there were courageous attempts to inaugurate manufactures as a partial offset to cotton culture, and a number of large yarn and cloth mills were established, but most of them languished. Anything requiring even the least amount of fabrication was apt to be procured from the North. Not only was it accepted that manufactures would not succeed in a plantation economy, but it was held that industry was inimical to the interests of slavery. Manufactures would import a sentiment favorable to a protective tariff, would divert capital and enterprise from acquisition of more lands and Negroes, and would set before the slaves the dangerous example of whole communities of poor men living by wages. It was recognized that manufactures represented a potential bond with the North, and this was shunned.

From this exclusive devotion to agriculture flowed poverty, a scattered and shifting population, ignorance, and a lack of participation of the majority of the people in social determinations, whether economic or political. There were purple patches of wealth in the hands of great planters or merchants, but their good fortune, materially or culturally, was not shared with the mass of the people. Their money was invested in an extension of the plantation system, or drew interest in the North and West. Most men had not the means to turn about, even had a spirit of enterprise possessed them. Even in prosperous districts, population was relatively sparse because of the size of farms and plantations, and on the fringe of these the Poor Whites, pushed out by slavery, lived meanly and precariously on sterile sandy ridges or in remote uplands. They subsisted on what they raised or shot or stole, and seldom came into contact with such sluggish trade currents as existed.

Moreover, the whole population felt the effects of the certain exhaustion of the soil under a one-crop system. There was a constant pull toward the virgin lands westward and southwestward. Impending removal, whether ever realized or not, infected every design. Why improve or remodel or fertilize or, least of all, embark upon a new business venture, when the next day or year might start a trek away from the wornout coastal lands? Household gods planted no "terrible fixed foot" and were uprooted without blood. The most affectionate attachments, out of which progress might have come in time, were wrenched loose by bankruptcy or by the division of slave property among younger sons outward bound.

Where the people were poor, scattered and impelled to move only by failure, ignorance followed as an inevitable consequence. William Gregg of South Carolina found that two-thirds of the Poor Whites could neither read nor write, the slaves were by law denied this knowledge, and even the sons of well-to-do families found poor facilities for study at home. There is reason to believe that in speaking of the aristocracy of the Old South we have too often confused culture with mere leisure.

Having nothing and knowing nothing, the mass of men could take no determining part in the public life of the South. Where they participated at all, they simply trudged in a column led by sloth, self-interest and caprice. When the agricultural tradition settled upon the South it had its exalters; when it was called into question, these became its loud defenders against all the world. Cotton culture with slave labor bred secession, and as abolition sentiment in the North nourished it, the Poor Whites became secessionists too. Their interests were all opposed to continuance of slavery, but they had no mind, no option but to follow the leader.

The restricted rôle of capital contributed to the absence of cities and towns and thus limited the division of labor. The progress of the South in recent years may be measured by the growth of urban population. Since the means for developing inventions were not available, these did not occur. Worst of all, from the standpoint of the South's preparation for its future, there was no wide-spread wage system. Afterwards, when industry was to be inaugurated, capital was accumulated and enterprisers appeared, as from the ground, to apply it to new projects; but the long absence of a cash relationship between worker and employer was not quickly remedied, to the detriment of the South today. Slaves were rationed, cabined and clothed; Poor Whites, except for a small number of artisans, were share-croppers or renters living on credit. So far as compensation was concerned, they were slaves too, except that in their case the planter or country merchant went through the form of keeping accounts in which their cotton or tobacco was set over against advances to them of calico, shoes, meat and molasses.

From all of this came a double behavior of the dominant whites toward poor men, whether white or black, namely, exploitation and patronage. They were to be used, not consulted; but they were to be used with kindness, even with sympathy. Their rights were defined in terms of responsibility of those who had for those who had not. If now and then acquisitiveness got the better of grace, only conscience stung, and conscience grew tolerant. Yet, *noblesse oblige* was a constituent part of the system which countenanced chattel slavery of the blacks and economic slavery of the whites. Nor was this just an accompaniment of blue blood, for men who knew they sat upon a volcano had reason to see that all proceeded gently.

The Civil War, of course, broke all bonds the South had had with the North and the nation; political allegiance severed, business connections abandoned, even church organizations split along sectional lines, were to be long in the repair. Secession now became not only a philosophy, but a passion for which men spent themselves.

Hardly had Appomattox marked the surrender of the Old South, when it was met with the lashes of Reconstruction, well laid on and received with bared back. Now the old creed, hallowed by defeat but really harmless enough, was shocked into renewed life by resentment. "The South in the Nation" had been the watchword of the conventions which forswore the ordinances of secession, but now "the South for the South" replaced it. This spirit has had its reverberations in our industrial development since the 'eighties after Reconstruction had passed.

The South has been unamenable to suggestions from without for industrial guidance, particularly in the matter of labor relations. We do not always remember how much of this is due to the South's belief that the North, by indulging in the rôle of lustful tyrant, sacrificed the confidence which it might have developed in its office of friendly critic.

These disabilities, inherited from the Old South, are deeply embedded in the New South. Only in the recent transition of the cotton manufacture in the South from sectional to national consequence, have these traits become critical. At first, and for years afterwards, all went blithely enough. After Reconstruction, in the late 'seventies and early 'eighties, a portion of the South, disaffected from the single pursuit of agriculture and eschewing politics as the only means of getting back at the North, embraced manufactures, particularly the spinning and weaving of cotton. The leaders in this new departure—F. W. Dawson, H. P. Hammett, G. A. Gray, D. A. Tompkins, to mention only a few—had many lieutenants and a host of followers. A campaign for the building of cotton factories enlisted press, pulpit and platform. A controversy over the relative cheapness of water and steam power was abandoned because even towns remote from waterfalls decided they must have mills anyhow.

The belief that proximity to the raw cotton was a patent advantage, has proved chimerical. But another native resource, the abundant labor supply found in the Poor Whites, proved a tremendous asset. It was everywhere pointed out that they would not only work for little, but that by the same sign it was charity to give them a livelihood. When it was known that a factory was to be built, families of Poor Whites in great numbers came to the site to engage jobs for themselves in advance. Almost in every case a village had to be erected to receive them. In some instances they actually stood about, waiting for the clapboards to be nailed to the studding. They came with nothing except children. In the case of a mill near Greenville, South Carolina, it was said that all of the spinning could have been done by three families!

The mill builders, directly or indirectly, wholly or in part, furnished every facility of life—work and wages, homes, churches, schools, stores. All was received with gratitude, as became families which had endured life at a minimum. Long hours, small pay, work of children day or night were taken as a matter of course. Nor did the employers have misgivings as to the consistency of their charity. They were creating an industry out of nothing, and were fearful that all might vanish before their eyes. How to get capital from a destitute South and an alienated North; how to market their product without serfdom to creditor commission men; how to take country peasants and give them skill to operate textile machinery—these were their problems. The general community was not concerned about low labor standards; remission of taxes for a term to encourage the location of a plant was general, enterprisers were cried up as messiahs, and the general public made itself an informal chamber of commerce to advance the industry. Founding of new factories and guaranty of success were the desiderata. Lack of wisdom in procedure and abstract injustice to the operative population were matters which, if they came to mind at all, could be taken care of later. Production was their palladium, as it was in the English Industrial Revolution a hundred years earlier.

Of course, it was exploitation of neglected resources—cotton, power, labor. When not only the stability but also the striking progress of the manufacturing venture became apparent, questionings arose as to the effects of industrialization upon the workers. A quarter-century after mills began to be built in numbers, child labor provoked attention, description, and plans of reform, both national and State. The eager but expiring voice of Edgar Gardner Murphy protested the plight of the child workers, and his cry was taken up by A. J. McKelway and Owen Lovejoy. The answer of the employers was in formal assertion of their patronal relation to their operatives. What at first had been a necessity of mill building, and a perfectly natural expression of the traditional responsibility of the master for his dependents, now became, on the part of many, a studied tactical pose. This pose has made progress *pari passu* with the growth of protest by or on behalf of labor. Welfare facilities of every description—social halls, swimming pools, cooking and sewing classes, equipment for athletic teams, pastures for cows, vacation camps—have been increased; this was particularly true during the World War when such a use of surplus profits served the double purpose of providing unction to the soul and cheating the tax gatherer. This deliberate adoption of the protective rôle by the employer is not undiluted, it must be said, by instances of ingenuous solicitude of mills for the well-being of their village populations.

So much for patronage, which is one horse in the span the Southern cotton manufacturers are driving. The other horse is exploitation. The indictment here is concerned primarily with hours and wages. The legal limit in South Carolina is 55 hours, in North Carolina and Georgia it is 60, and Alabama has no legal limit. Every Southern State permits night work for women, and the 11-hour day six days a week, and the 12-hour night five nights a week are common. In the South generally children of 14 may work the same hours as adults. Alabama is an exception to this rule, and there is an unimportant educational requirement in North Carolina. Average full-time hours in the five leading Southern States—North and South Carolina, Georgia, Virginia and Alabama—were in 1928, according to Bureau of Labor Statistics figures taken by the sampling method, 55.4 as against 51.9 for the five leading New England

States. In 1926 the hours in the South were 55.58, and in New England 51.24. Massachusetts has a legal limit of 48 hours, with a prohibition upon night work for women, which means that the mills are unable to operate a night shift.

There are several ways of stating wages. If we divide the total wage bill for the year by the average number of workers, we get an approximation of average annual earnings, a slight error being due to the fact that some manufacturers report only for weeks in which their plants are in full operation. By this method the average weekly earnings in the five leading Southern States in 1927 were $12.94. In the five leading New England States they were $19.12, or 47.8 per cent greater. The latest official figures are those of the United States Bureau of Labor Statistics for 1928, taken by the sampling method. These figures show that the five leading Southern States average full-time weekly wages of $15.24, and that the five leading New England States average $20.11. On the other hand, average actual weekly earnings (not average full time) were, according to the Bureau, $10.98 in the five Southern States and $17.15 in those of New England.

Lower wages and longer hours are the principal items contributing to the lower cost of manufacturing cotton in the South as compared with the North. According to the study made in 1926 by Main and Gunby, of the American Society of Mechanical Engineers, a typical Southern mill running 55 hours had a manufacturing cost which was 16.8 per cent less than a Massachusetts mill running 48 hours; this difference amounted to $6.73 per spindle, of which $4.53 was attributable to saving in labor. Where the Southern mill maintained a company-owned village the differential was cut to 14 per cent.

It is commonly said in extenuation of the low absolute wage paid in the South that the cost of living is enough lower than in the North to bring real wages to a parity. Estimates of the amount the Southern operative receives in wholesale prices and other mill-village benefits run all the way from $8 per week down to $3.46, the figure furnished by the American Cotton Manufacturers' Association. Main and Gunby thought the Southern manufacturer spent $1.13 per spindle per year on his mill-village over and above similar charges upon the Northern manufacturer, or about one-eighth of the wage bill in the South. On the basis of a weekly wage of $12.94 in the five leading Southern States, this amounts to an added wage to the operative of $1.62.

The National Industrial Conference Board made studies of the cost of living of cotton-mill employes in New England and Southern textile centers in 1919 and 1920. The figures are old, but remain the best available. The studies sought to ascertain the cost of maintaining " a minimum but reasonable standard of living for a representative wage-earner's family " in Lawrence and Fall River, Massachusetts, in Greenville and Pelzer, South Carolina, and in Charlotte, North Carolina. The items involved were not precisely the same, because of differences in food habits, but every effort was made to have them comparable. The results showed, to the surprise of many, that for a family living in Greenville and Charlotte, even considering the low rates paid for shelter, fuel and light, the cost of living was higher than in Fall River and Lawrence: in Greenville it was $1393.60 yearly; in Charlotte, $1438.03; in Fall River, $1267.76; in Lawrence, $1385.78; and in Pelzer, a typical isolated mill village, $1374.09. If the family did not live in a company house in Charlotte, the cost, $1525.67, was much higher than in the North. Comparing Lawrence and Greenville, the Northern and Southern points closest together in cost of living of an operative family, the saving in the item of shelter in Greenville, $137.28, was a little more than offset by the greater cost of food, $143.00; clothing cost $16.89 more in Greenville than in Lawrence. Fuel and sundries also cost slightly more in the Southern textile center.

The " stretch-out " system was the match which set off the powder train of strikes in the cotton-mill South. This means simply that operatives are required to tend an increased number of machines, generally looms. It is reported that an increase of from 24 to 76 looms per man has been common. Of course extra assistance is given the weaver, but the intent is to cut down the labor cost per unit of product. In an extreme case, on the coarsest goods, weavers are reported to be running 140 looms. Back of the stretch-out lie, of course, the low labor standards prevailing in the South, for these were a potent factor in giving the New England industry hard sledding; indeed, this condition resulted in the introduction of the stretch-out in those Northern factories remaining in their old setting, and in the importation of the plan to the South when others migrated.

In the middle of April, 1929, there were 17,000 or 18,000 men out on account of strikes in the Carolinas and Tennessee. This was the numerical peak, though the controversies grew in intensity with the occurrence of shootings in Gastonia and Marion, North Carolina, in June and October, and of beatings and various forms of mob violence in the months between. Of the three prominent strikes, at Gastonia, Elizabethton and Marion, the first was led by the National Textile Workers' Union, a Communist organization existing entirely on paper, and the other two by the United Textile Workers, affiliated with the American Federation of Labor. The so-called leaderless strikes in South Carolina, which were of short duration, met with slight concessions or resulted in a return to work on the old basis.

The employers in the South, in defending themselves before public opinion, have been prompted by and have relied upon the tradition of Southern suspicion against the North. Implied in much that they have said and done has been the notion that their industrial efforts mean progress for the South, and that labor demands are inspired in the North. In good part this is disingenuous, but it still makes its appeal. The beset mills have intrenched themselves, also, behind their welfare work as proof of their solicitude for their workers. The public mind of the South is still content with social subsidy, but here and there, particularly in the more liberal attitude of important newspapers toward the recent disturbances, there appears evidence of a demand for social justice. A legislative committee in South Carolina very early in the recent strikes laid the whole trouble to overwork and underpayment of the operatives; the Southern Industrial Council, composed of middle-class liberals, has taken the same stand; Southerners appeared before the Senate Committee on Manufactures to ask for an investigation of the American textile industry with a view to showing evils in the South and, if possible, pointing a way out; the Southern cotton manufacturers' trade journal hitherto most Bourbon in its support of the mills, has now begun to chide the employers for overstepping prudence in the introduction of the stretch-out. There have been fewer evictions this time than ever 'before. On the other hand, troops have been called out almost as often in the strikes of the past spring and summer as in the whole previous history of the cotton-mill strikes in the South.

This awakening recognition has been hindered by the killing of a police chief and seven strikers and the wounding of others, with the consequent trials.

It is lamentable that the fanfare of emotional protest has been flung up to obscure the industrial issues. Invective, reproaches and bitterness have been enemies to the calm thinking which is necessary where sharp conflict has sprung up in a section new to manufactures and newer to class cleavage. Gory particulars of gas bombs and pistol bullets, while inevitable accompaniments of such a struggle, do little to bring adjustment or solution.

Southern operatives in the past have responded in large numbers to appeals of organizers to join the union, but their adherence has come only at times of special drives, and has been brief. In recent months, however, there have been spontaneous strikes, which, while not unknown before, as at Henderson, North Carolina, in 1927, this time have shown the novel character of ability to spread and become consecutive. There has been more local leadership in these strikes than ever before in the textile South. The Piedmont Organizing Council, which in frequent educational meetings in the last year has been preaching the doctrine of unionism, has been essentially a Southern enterprise. The organization of the moderate United Textile Workers gains by comparison with the Communist National Textile Workers; the demands of the latter at Gastonia for an eight-hour day, 20-dollar wage and recognition of the union, were courageous and, at least abstractly, reasonable; but rightly or wrongly, their strike has been branded with having less solici-

THE PROBLEM

tude for betterment of Southern workers than for advancement of Communist propaganda. Southern employers have regularly said in the past that the American Federation of Labor union was inspired from Moscow; now that real Communists have come on the scene, the conservative union grows in respectability.

The method of labor organization in Southern mills heretofore has been that of infrequent campaigns in which large numbers were swept into the union, only to see membership dwindle afterwards in the face of half-hearted nursing of the locals. This was expensive and ineffective, though, as workers carried their stories in their shiftings from mill to mill, it did leave a lingering tradition of unionism in many villages. Miss MacDonald, talking with operatives in villages in the Carolinas not long before the recent strikes, found many who held organization to be the right and the salvation of the Southern workers.

The last wave of strikes may be said to have caught the unions unawares, unless, perhaps, the National Textile Workers did some prior organizing in Gastonia. One outburst followed another with such rapidity that there was little opportunity for planning, even had the leaders been able to snatch their attention away from the problem of raising money.

Many feel now, after ten months of sensational strikes, that the South has been brought squarely into the current of national economic controversy. There is wide-spread conviction that improvement of labor standards in the textile South constitutes the most pressing task before the American labor movement. What will be the plan of organization in the future? Two methods present themselves.

The American Federation of Labor at its convention in Toronto in October, resolved to throw its weight behind a united drive along the entire Southern front. This policy is supported by those who have been critical of the piecemeal tactics of the old line Federation leaders in the past. Their advocacy is a natural enough deduction from unfortunate experience heretofore. Also, they want to strike a resounding blow with a big sledge while the iron is hot. They remember well that raps of the hammer here and there have accomplished little or nothing. They do not believe that the bundle of sticks can be taken apart and broken one by one. They would assail the unity.

I believe that this method has little to recommend it, that it will be abandoned on reflection. In the first place, textile workers the country over are only about four per cent organized, and never had, even at the peak in 1920, more than 15 per cent membership in the union. There are only about 10,000 cotton-mill workers organized out of some half million in the country; over half of this total number of operatives is in the South, where, as we have seen, only a beginning toward unionization has been made. Less than one-third of the members of the chief union, the United Textile Workers, are cotton-mill hands. At the very time when the union needs to summon its strength for the Southern task, it is losing membership and morale by the decay of the industry in its Northern stronghold. Furthermore, there is dissension within the ranks of organized textile workers; the United, while most important, shares the field with other organizations on craft and geographical lines, besides encountering the violent opposition of periodic risings of Communists and others as at Gastonia. Thus the nucleus around which to rally a big united drive is itself on the anxious seat.

What does a resolution of the American Federation of Labor mean, besides good intent? The Federation itself has no authority over the constituent unions. It can only use persuasion and pass the hat. This will net something as long as excitement in the South continues, but it is not the source of funds for a long-drawn and expensive organizing campaign. The history of the steel strike of 1919-20 proves as much, and that was an easier task than the present one.

The Southern cotton manufacturers are worried, but they are compactly organized in a South-wide and in State associations, and the Cotton Textile Institute, which was set up to solve the problems of the industry, by its own constitution is prevented from interfering with the different labor costs in the South. The Southern employers make a more formidable opposition to union effort than those more accustomed to fighting labor organizations; there are among them virtually none who sees advantages in dealing with unions, and they are sufficiently inexperienced to be sustained by the belief that they will be able to hold the South as a fortress against unionism. They are ready to give united support to the first of their number who is attacked, and to visit him with killing blows, should he yield. Against such an enemy only a large membership in the union involved, with great financial reserves behind it, can be successfully pitted.

It is true, however, that the announced union method of concerted assault has this to recommend it, namely, that competition in the cotton-manufacturing industry, particularly as between mills making the same product, is so keen that a single company pressed into concessions to labor is victimized; it is desirable to raise the level of wages and to decrease the number of hours in as many mills as possible at the same time. This was the secret of success through the method of factory legislation used in England in the last century; ten hours, unless under exceptional circumstances, would have sunk any mill until all were forced to conform to it.

The other plan is that of gradual infiltration, and it is my opinion that this is the method which practical experience will soon endorse. Its object will be to organize in a few mills at a time, with little said about demands. That it is not necessary, for organization purposes, to make demands that will be costly to the employer if acceded to, is shown by the number of recent strikes in which the chief fight was against discrimination. The union's aim with the employer will be for recognition and the establishment of confidence. Mindful of small profit margins, it will be content with relatively minor adjustments in working conditions. It will aim to prove to the employer that it is a constructive organ, with his interest as well as the workers' at heart.

The union will discern that what the Southern employer stands most in need of is education. Once the union is in a position where it can work with an employer, it may address itself to the task of getting what improvement it may in that mill by cooperation with him, and then reach over to another plant. So far as I know, there is not a single cotton factory in the South which regularly deals with the union. There is not one "union employer." What the union needs in the South, in its weak condition, is some friends among the employers, some who recognize that the union is not a tyrant, but a protector—a protector against walkouts, violence, hastily patched up and as hastily broken agreements, suspended dividends and the hard feelings and downright difficulties attendant upon evictions.

When a foothold is gained in one place, a start may be made in another. The favorable experience of the first manufacturer will be a recommendation to the second. Membership in the union will have grown. Union plants will provide lodgment for men on strike elsewhere. The Southern employer is not afraid of the constructive unionism represented by the United Textile Workers; he is afraid of a bogey which he has erected before his own eyes. Once he touches the bogey or knows the experience of a fellow employer who has touched it, its terrors will be largely dispelled. All will not go blithely, but at first patiently and then more swiftly, opposition in the textile South to the idea of unionism as predatory and unAmerican will be dissipated. Circumstances will encourage the prosecution of more vigorous measures. For one thing, public opinion will be readier in support of restrictive legislation. For another, as more and more mills drift southward, the section will produce a greater variety of goods, and the competition among great numbers of mills making identical products will be more and more diluted. More skill will be developed in manufacture—not a little through greater proficiency of unionized operatives—and in distribution and sales. We shall see more of such successful efforts as the recent one to market fine cottons for women's clothing.

Organized labor, if it is to prosper in the South, must attach the intelligentsia to its cause. The South scarcely has an aristocracy of wealth, but it still has a powerful aristocracy of culture and social idealism. This aristocracy, in which churchmen figure importantly, will not be won over by shock and outrage, but by a reasonable and circumspect advance in labor organization. The doctrine of States' Rights has already taken on the better habit of pride in the State's fair dealing. This has shown itself in the recent strikes.

Reprobating the failure to indict the murderers of a striker after seven Communists had been sentenced for the shooting of the chief of police, the Raleigh *News and Observer* said: " Gaston county in the eyes of fair-minded, justice-loving, intelligent people the world over is indicted as a county in which one Ella May more or less doesn't matter and in which justice is the harlot of hate and prejudice and hysteria and industrial wrong." This is one such expression in many. As yet the South's social conscience may be stirred only over killings and the like, but it will learn to protest effectively against the deeper but less sensational wrongs of day-by-day industrial exploitation. And the workers themselves, who as yet have done no autonomous thinking, will begin to second this protest with native voice. The English cotton mill workers, of the same stock, went through all this, and now, though their industry is in worse plight than ours, they are 75 per cent organized, and have a constructive and cooperative part in all great decisions affecting the manufacture there.

The Southern mills are standardized as to equipment, and too standardized as to product, but they can stand much improvement in elimination of waste (consider only absenteeism of workers), in which an organized labor force may have a hand. The wisest do not see far into the ultimate method of remedying low wages and long hours in the South as a part of a depressed national and world industry, but no likely calculation will reckon without organized self-expression for the workers.

2. FLESHPOTS IN THE SOUTH [1]

The notion has long prevailed that the South is peculiar. New England, the Middle West, the Northwest, and the Pacific Slope have their characteristics, but these have been accepted as products of physical environment and economic pursuit, and have not been considered ingrained genius of the people. In the latter sections changes have taken place. New England has shifted from farming to commerce and so to industry; from a huntsman's frontier the West has become a " producing interior " for foodstuffs and manufactures; on the Pacific, fruit growing and ocean shipping have been added to mining; all populations have been on the move, bloodstrains altering, and, through discovery of ore and oil deposits, extension of railways and development of irrigation, new enterprise has been invited.

[1] April, 1927.

Nobody was surprised if other regions shifted political allegiance, showed novel industrial adventure or made fresh contribution in art or literature. Such things are the products of American communities in process of growth. But the Southern tradition has been viewed as fixed. New employments might enter, unwonted alignment of classes might be suggested, but these only slightly modified the essential nature of Southern society. There was a presiding spirit in the people which rendered them superior to external influences and set them apart as belonging to a distinct culture.

Southerners have been foremost in putting forward this view of themselves. What we have made a fetish others have been willing to accept as a fact. We have constantly used the theory of peculiarity as an alibi, to make light of lack of accomplishment or to defend departures from national practice. Even when the Union forced the abolition of slavery, the discipline was not sufficient to stop the defiant protest of innocence or to stamp out the disturbing sense of martyrdom. We have not been distinguished for critical faculty. We have been romanticists rather than realists.

It is universal knowledge that the South is making spectacular strides economically. The rush to Florida and the diffusion of the speculators as they drifted out of the peninsula has brought suddenly to the attention of the country changes which had long been in process. The southward drift of the cotton manufacturing industry has produced resounding yelps of pain from New England. Everyone begins to speak of Birmingham in the same breath with Pittsburgh and Gary. Muscle Shoals and the Catawba River power dams are great units in a new national resource. North Carolina bond issues to build thousands of miles of perfect roads have captured the imagination of the continent. Securities of Southern railroads are bid for by every investor. The South is news for every editor. Magazines devote issues to proclaiming fresh achievements from the Potomac to the Gulf.

The question now is whether these great industrial developments will banish the personality of the South as we have known it, or whether the old spirit will actuate the new performance. Will industrialism produce the same effects here as elsewhere, or will it submit to be modified by a persistent Southern termperament? Will an underlying culture prove superior to changed economic pursuits?

Almost fifty years ago when the term "New South" was popularized by Henry W. Grady and others, many decried its use if by the phrase the death of the Old South was implied. And in the years since then writers have attempted to show not only that the Southern tradition has been continuous, but that industry itself has exhibited, except for the interruption of the Civil War, a steady growth.

To take the second of these contentions first. In the ante-bellum South a slothful, wasteful agriculture predominated. There were a few iron furnaces and little cotton yarn factories, but they were small neighborhood affairs, for the most part supplying a local market; they were frequently worked by slaves and often gave their products in barter. William Gregg, who built his cotton mill at Graniteville, South Carolina, in the late 'forties, is almost the sole figure who compared with Northern manufacturers of the period. In organizing ability, in grasp of the South's economic problems and in eagerness to save the South by introduction of industrial activity he was remarkable, and his crusade had results which might have been of dynamic importance had not the system against which he worked proved too strong for him.

The Civil War cut short these beginnings. When, following Reconstruction, the campaign to "bring the cotton mill to the cotton field" enlisted wide support, the movement was an entirely new one. If there was a hold-over from Gregg's day, even, it was not conspicuous. A few men who figured in the later period were connected, in one way and another, with the old factories; George A. Gray, who was the pioneer of the great development at Gastonia, had worked as a boy in the little mill at Pinhook near by, and H. P. Hammett, who built the Piedmont Mill in the 'seventies, was the son-in-law of an ante-bellum manufacturer. But for the most part the boom swept into cotton manufacturing any and all who had the confidence of their communities. It was a new gospel. The will to be saved was more important than previous experience.

Nor does the spirit of the old South survive in the new day which confronts us now. The industrial enterprisers of the 'eighties and 'nineties, while borrowing little of manufacturing practice from ante-bellum years, were in many cases men of honorable tradition. They showed extraordinary economic suppleness in taking the lead in unaccustomed projects. Adhering to an old code, they functioned in a changed environment. They were used to assuming responsibility. They were proud of their families. They were mindful of the esteem in which they were held. Slavery had taught them to be fatherly toward those dependent upon them. They had always been resourceful, and the havoc of war could not destroy their self-confidence. They had fought in gray jacket and red shirt to preserve the South, and now, if manufacturing was the right way out for their people, they would learn to produce yarn and cloth. With the hope of personal profit playing no mean part, it is still not too much to say that giving employment to the Poor Whites became their passion. Just as the villein of the Middle Ages rendered unquestioned service if only he could build his thatched hut in the shadow of the lord's castle, so the Poor Whites flocked from mountain side and tenant holding to enter new factory villages where they received the first protection they had known. Management and men were drawn together in the closest ties, because all alike were investing their last fervent hopes in a strange adventure. Moreover, New England mocked. The South manufacture cotton? The thing was ridiculous. Where was the capital, the skill, the labor? Could gentlemen turn factory superintendents? Could degenerate squirrel-shooters and bilious share-croppers learn to tend looms and frames? And this raillery solidified Southern energy; the toes of socks were searched to find money to buy shares of mill stock on instalments; and besides, some willing allies were found at the North—machinery men and commission firms which stood to profit by advancing equipment and credit.

These leaders in the first twenty years of the South's manufacturing development were not working in a normal industrial order. They were not faced with many problems of competition. Despite the rise of cotton mills in the South, the Northern factories continued prosperous. It was two decades before the United States census, for example, attached much importance to the Southern growth from a national standpoint. Such change as was effected in the North was in a gradual shifting away from coarse goods manufacture, in which Southerners had differential advantage. The counterpart of this inter-sectional freedom was intra-sectional peace. There was no cleavage between owners and operatives. They did not see themselves as employers and employes, but as companions in the same boat on rather desperate seas. If anything besides joint economic effort were needed to weld them into one, the presence of the free blacks accomplished it. Cotton manufacturing, a providential escape from jeopardy, was to remain a white man's industry. Moreover, managers and men were of one blood and, essentially, of one tradition. The Poor Whites had always hated Negroes rather than their owners, and the trials of Reconstruction had wiped out lingering enmities. Therefore, as Whites and as Southerners and as injured and poor men, all were partners in enterprise. Long hours, low wages and early work of children did not even arouse comment for many years, and realization of a " cash nexus " did not become articulate until the late 'nineties.

These industrial leaders in the South in the opening decades were of a different stripe from most of the cotton manufacturers, mine owners and iron masters who figured in the English Industrial Revolution. The former were gentlemen, the latter were small men who struck it lucky. Only such exceptional individuals as Robert Owen, Richard Arkwright and Samuel Oldknow, who were philanthropists while they were employers, were of the same temper with the first Southerners. In New England the rigors of the outset of factory employment had been softened by such a benevolent proprietor as Francis Lowell. But just as in Old England and New England, gain got the better of generosity, so in the South the second generation of manufacturers chose speedily to hunt with the hounds.

In fact, they are industrialists, business men, capitalists, and congratulate themselves upon supporting these characters. They are not subject to the restraints of their fathers. They do not have an emotional attitude toward their workers. They are not burdened with a sense of *noblesse oblige*. They are not aristocrats, but bourgeois. They are classconscious and money-wise.

One could overlook a natural lack of economic breadth if only they were honest. They have sought to cloak their materialism with a great show of philanthropy and social conscience. Qualities which in their fathers were spontaneous and meaningful, they have laid claim to and adapted to their uses. They have built up a program of welfare work in the villages which is the last word in the furnishing of health and social facilities to employes. They subsidize schools and churches and Young Men's Christian Associations; they build recreation centers and moving picture houses and swimming pools; they furnish doctors and nurses; they maintain libraries and dairies and brass bands. There is some good will in all of this, and in particular instances it is mostly good will, but generally speaking the welfare program is prosecuted because it pays.

You would never think so to listen to these mill men. In their accounts human kindness is the overwhelming motive. They assert that the South, always different from the rest of the country, more spirituelle and more idealistic, is showing a new reaction under industrialism. Manufacturing development is not to repeat in the South the history it has had elsewhere. The familiar phenomena of bitterness and exploitation, they declare, do not figure in this favored section. Witness the way in which a Charlotte trade journal sought to neutralize the movement for national child labor legislation by publishing at strategic moments, " Health and Happiness " numbers, showing little girls in sashes scampering about May poles!

This is pure cant. If you thrust your fingers into the downy wool of the lamb you feel beneath it the coarse bristle of the wolf. The employers, certainly in the cotton manufacturing business, have tried to make their private interests appear as synonymous with the well-being of society, and have very largely succeeded. The ministers supported by manufacturers have, as a rule, no independence of mind. Religion, as one observer has said, is administered to operatives like a drug. Welfare agents, when it comes to the test, are wholly the servants of management. The schools do not emphasize, if they so much as discuss, the economic issues every day present and pressing.

What is true of the company-dominated villages is also true of social institutions in the wider community. Legislature, press, pulpit and platform subscribe to the employer's creed of disingenuous individualism. Yet in the wider sense this is not altogether, or even mainly, a result of the direct influence of the Southern business man of today. He himself and all the agencies which speak with him are products of a stage of economic evolution. The South, despite every denial, is showing all the well-known consequences of industrial growth, and the unconscious elements in the situation declare this fact most eloquently. Did not the English manufacturers of the Industrial Revolution proclaim that private interest was identical with public benefit? However compensated for or glossed over, wages are low and hours are long. Unionism is greeted by employers with abuse. It is effrontery, a pernicious piece of presumption, a cancer in the industrial body, and is always a foreign importation—if not from the jealous North, then proceeding immediately from Bolshevist Russia itself. Unionism would never be born in the minds of the satisfied, right-thinking native workers. Strikes are put down ruthlessly, with eviction, starvation, militia, spies, and effective cooperation between employers. The sop of company unionism is thrown to the workers, with every effort to make this move appear as a progressive philanthropy. Anent the sessions of the American Plan Open Shop Conference in Dallas in November, the Manufacturers' Record said: "To the South . . . this meeting will be of peculiar significance and importance as the South now appears to be the only corner of the country not yet harried by the warfare of organized labor against the unorganized people of the nation.''

In wider public expression the same spirit is manifest. A map of the country showing the progress of workmen's compensation legislation shows the South as the backward provinces. The solid South offered the greatest bloc of opposition to the child labor amendment to the constitution. The shibboleth of States' Rights was disinterred and held up before the country as the high principle animating the South's objection. In this case as in that of slavery, the use of States' Rights, where not a device of corruption, was the sign of a depth of ignorance even more lamentable. Western farmers were organized against the amendment by a North Carolina textile trade journal. The same men who a few years ago were protesting against State legislative interference with labor conditions represented themselves, when truly effective federal law impended, as wedded to the principle of careful control by the individual commonwealth. There was no subtle engineering, no fine Italian hand in maneuver. The awkward driving fist of capitalism pushed at every point, without so much as the saving grace of consistency, but only the thinly disguised force of a greedy interest.

The Poor Whites, who at the outset of the cotton mill era in the South were cherished and by whose labor the industry has been built up, are now looked upon as a resource to be exploited. Not only is this true within the section, but the Poor Whites are being served up to employers of the country who may be tempted to locate plants in the South. The workers are being offered on the auction block pretty much as their black predecessors were, and their qualities are enlarged upon with the same salesman's gusto. Native Whites! Anglo-Saxons of the true blood! All English-speaking! Tractable, harmonious, satisfied with little! They know nothing of foreign-born radicalism! Come down and gobble them up! Trade papers advertise them, chambers of commerce sound their convenient virtues. Hear Mr. Edgerton, a Southerner and president of the National Association of Manufacturers: " This population is preponderantly native. It is a native soil in which exotic radicalism does not thrive, for the worker of the South has as a heritage a sturdy Americanism that restrains him from running after strange economic gods and makes him a dependable factor in industry."

Everybody recognizes that the chief advantage which the South possesses in cotton manufacturing in particular, but in other industries as well, lies in cheap labor. There are other items of importance—abundant power, a wealth of raw materials, up-to-date management, lenient taxation, genial climate—but the great differential is in low wages paid to submissive workers. What is the attitude of the Northern manufacturers who enter the Southern field? In two years, it is calculated, they invested

$100,000,000 in 1,000,000 Southern spindles. They know perfectly well why they come, and they intend to make the most of the opportunity before them. Lockwood, Greene & Company, great New England cotton mill engineers and manufacturers giving ever increasing attention to the Southern field, were recently asked for a statement of the advantages offered by this region. Everyone concerned for the people of the South must resent the reply: "As compared to New England and the Northeastern part of the country, the South has the advantage of longer hours of labor, lower wage scales, lower taxes, and legislation which gives a manufacturing plant a wider latitude than is usually possible in the North in the way of running over-time and at night . . . The South is . . . fortunate in having a supply of native American labor which is still satisfied to work at a low wage." Here is naïveté, but also that cruelty which has earned hatred for capitalism. The South is now being visited by an elemental economic force, the search of a world industry for an area of cheap labor. The present rush to the cotton states is but an episode. Will Asia be next?

Newcomers have always been quick to profess loyalty to the Southern tradition—like other apostates, they are more ardent than believers to the manner born. In the past, firms with plants in both sections have submitted to an advanced labor code in New England while arguing for laxness in the South. Only in the last few years have they come out boldly when, for example, petitioning the legislature of Massachusetts to let down the bars in order that the industry there may survive the killing competition of the Southern States. Southern churches and colleges have not borne an honorable part in the problems brought by the new industrialism. Both have been soaked with evangelism, and this has not made for the defining or even the realization of issues. In a broad view this behavior has not been their fault. Simon N. Patten was right when he said that a society on a deficit basis produces a religion of fear and of asceticism, but not of enterprise and courage. When the South was desperately poor, men's minds flew to the thought of salvation through denial. The great virtue was to suffer and do without, while cultivating spiritual purity. Sufficiency of economic goods appearing impossible, it was looked upon as a profanation. To the extent that physical well-being was striven for, it was to be got through loyalty to one another and should be received with humble thanksgiving.

Now that Southern society is entering into a surplus of wealth, the old motives are, unfortunately, slow to relax their grip. We see in a mirror, darkly, and rarely face to face. We do not recognize evidences of the changing order which are commonplaces elsewhere. The pity of fundamentalism is not that it clings to the Garden of Eden. That point of conflict is of trifling and transitory importance. But to the extent that the doctrine holds sway it argues

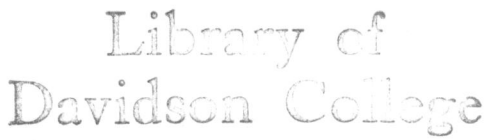

ignorance of the principle of growth in social institutions; being religious fundamentalists, we declare ourselves lay fundamentalists as well. Industrialism, however, is precipitating in the South a whole series of imperative new moralities, and we are not readjusting our sanctions to meet them. If ministers are still obsessed with faith and piety and strained with mental anguish, teachers confuse issues with an elaborate overlay of sociological metaphysics. Religion plays a stronger part with them than science; emotion is more potent than analysis. Has either the church or the college shown leadership of the South in the maze presented by industrial advance? We speak strongly of the necessity of courage on the part of Southern teachers in the social sciences. How many sought to direct the public thought on the important question of national control over child labor?

The day when preachers and pedagogues dedicated themselves to the salvation of a backward South is passing. We need to be more objective, more pragmatic. Material prosperity is putting the South on a parity with the rest of the world. Pulpit and classroom can fill their best office now by being critical rather than compassionate. The bedside manner should be dropped for straightforward diagnosis. The old conjure is discredited. If the South is by any chance to escape certain of the ill effects that have marked the course of industrialism elsewhere, it is to be by hushing the ancient incantation of a persistent Southern tradition, and seeing ourselves in the flat light of historical experience. A move in this direction has been made by the University of North Carolina, and the need for it is shown by the fire immediately drawn from the cotton manufacturers of the State.

A Baltimore minister has recently denounced the economic interpretation of history as damnable. Nevertheless, all in the South except a tiny minority can see now that it was an economic system which drew us, with labored justifications thrust before, into the Civil War. How long will it take us to comprehend that industrial forces are shaping Southern life of today?

It is inevitable that a great new urge from farming toward industry should color and presently determine the culture of the people. If it is possible to shape industrial practice deliberately, or to direct the development of social institutions, we must at least know the history of similar societies in the past. We must be historically conscious. In this historical awareness the South is conspicuously lacking, and most of all the spokesmen for the business community itself.

The theory that the South is peculiar is at variance with the facts. I have been reading the confession of faith, covering 15 years' activity, of the editor of the *Southern Textile Bulletin*. This story of exultant opposition to protective labor legislation and labor organization is an amazing recital. It would need a very superficial glance to wave it aside as the effort of a special pleader to curry favor with profit-seeking advertisers on whose patronage the journal depends for its life. To the student of economic history it is first of all a declaration of ignorance. Before me is also Samuel Kydd's *History of the Factory Acts*. The two present a parallel perfect to the last particular. The struggle of collective welfare against individualistic design in the South was acted out, speech by speech, scene by scene, a century earlier in England. Substitute Murphy, McKelway and Lovejoy for Sadler, Oastler and Shaftesbury, and put Smyth and Clark in the places of Cobden and Graham and it immediately strikes home that the advocates of our time, both for and against, have been the products of an economic process.

The same arguments, evasions, tricks, the same words make up the two stories. To go a little further back, there was the Southern Gregg to match the British Owen. Substitute the name of Graniteville for that of New Lanark and you do no violence to the facts of early welfare work in a factory village. The president of the Southern Textile Social Service Association is " anxious that the development of the industry and the changes accompanying continue to be controlled by (*sic*) a result of conscious planning rather than unconscious drifting." Yet the industry does drift because the rudder of perspective has been lacking to the manufacturers and to the community which should steer them. Why kick against the pricks? Robert Owen was right. We are creatures of circumstance, unless we lay hold vigorously upon education. If other proof in the case of the South were wanting, consider with what accuracy the Irishman Cairnes, supplied by Olmsted with a few basic economic facts, pictured forth what must be the nature of Southern society under slavery. Helper, in the midst of what was happening, did not achieve a more accurate account. From disturbances in the motion of Uranus, LeVerrier described the planet Neptune which he could not see.

Industrialism, with its concomitants, will, soon or late, appeal to everyone as the most potent fact in the life of the South since emancipation of the slaves. In many respects the second is a more fundamental change than the first. The passing of slavery left us the Negro still a serf wholly dependent and playing the same old rôle in a predominantly agricultural order. Nominally his status was different, but practically it was the same. The Poor White still had to meet black competition. The upper whites—expropriated, humiliated—were in worse case than before to act the part of social solvents.

But manufacturing was begun and, though effects showed themselves only slowly, a real hope for the future of the South had dawned. For many years while industry was in its incipiency, the South followed the tradition it had known, that of agonizing over present difficulties and praying for future adjustments. There was much weariness of the flesh and vexation of the spirit. We lashed ourselves to unavailing heroisms. We sat in sack-cloth and ashes and, like Job, boasted our woes. Or we invoked Heaven to send a miracle to release us, and there was no answering voice. We were trying to lift ourselves by our bootstraps. The disappearance of distrust of the North, the banishment of illiteracy, the bettering of farm methods, the enlivening of country life, the improvement of the Negro's lot could not be wrought through a hocus-pocus.

All of these consummations waited upon a very material thing—the accumulation of wealth. If wishes were horses, beggars would ride. Now the horses are here. A more generous basis of taxation speeds the spread of schools. The coming of cotton mill communities carries the Poor Whites, in seven-league boots, from stagnating isolation to participation in a busy progress. Restriction upon immigration does more for the Negro in a decade—opening to him steel mills and automobile plants and a thousand other avenues of employment—than a generation of interracial conferences could accomplish.

The plight of the cotton grower is not resolvable except through industrialism. Extension agencies, government bureaus, valorization, cooperative selling, rural credits are all limited by the incurable individualism of the farmer. The retributive justice of low prices is cruel in the process but kinder in the end. Why prolong the agony of marginal producers? When they give up and go to cotton mill work they gain and those left in the country gain. The mill village has not been an unmixed blessing, but still it is, more than any other one thing, the road to freedom. The cotton manufacture is now attracting its proper accessory industries. Lumbering, mining, construction and transportation, iron, tobacco and fertilizer works offer alternative employments, and the South approaches release from the lop-sided economic development from which most of her woes have sprung.

The South a champion of fundamentalism? Why, it is the world's chief evidence in our day of the compelling power of evolution! In 1900 only 14 per cent of the South's population was urban. Now 25 per cent of Southerners live in cities. Cities and all they imply will be the death of the fundamentalist superstition. Cities mean variety of work, keenness of competition, sharpening of wits, relief in amusements. Cities are tossing streams running away to the open sea. They have left behind the headless, slimy ponds of the back country. Cities represent works rather than faith.

Only to the superficially spiritual does all this activity in the South appear as materialistic. Probably there were some with Joshua who refused to enter the promised land, and would fain go back to be buried with Moses. But the chastening of desert years ought to lend a finer appreciation of our new flowing land. All that was best in the South of yesterday is needed in the South of today and tomorrow.

Even accepting the view of pessimists, did the old South have so much to offer that we should regret its passing? Viewed honestly, what was it? A frontier community, with a degree of luxury for a tiny minority resting upon social starvation for a subjected majority. Such a scheme of things might be expected to produce some few elegancies. Czarist Russia did as much, or more. Something precious perished when the family of Nicholas was shot down. Turkey had its divans and pillows and perfumes. "Still," the doubter says, "there has always been an unique inescapable *something* in the Southern people, in all the Southern people." I wonder if there has been. There was, for long, inescapable poverty, and ignorance, and lack of opportunity. There was a deceptive loyalty on the part of the masses to the very agencies of their oppression. There was hospitality for strangers, but this has been the universal accompaniment, the world over, of sparse settlement. Warmth of meeting did not extend itself to new ideas.

No, it is not the New South which is on trial, but the old. Industry below the Potomac is in adolescence, it is true. It flouts its elders, it distorts values, it mocks with its self-assurance. But it will soon be growing to manhood, and will bring up with it the whole of the South—calm, matured, and, be it hoped, resourceful—for the first time established as a part of the American achievement. Industrialism, though alien, is the instrument of Southern salvation. Joseph, carried off into Egypt, succored his brethren.

3. Southern Spindles [1]

We were awakened by a scuffling and thumping on the old stairs. Labored breathing sounded through the door, which after a moment lurched open. A giant Negro stood over us. He had a wooden leg. This timber seemed as large as one of the props under his log cabin behind the " big house." In these degenerate plantation days, " Peg " combined the functions of out-Negro and body-servant. While he poured out the shaving water he took orders from my host about the feeding of the mules. It was Sunday, and they might have the new green feed, the first of the spring.

After breakfast we watched those gaunt plough-pullers at their feast. Their tender must have his holiday too; so he used his immemorial right of hitching one of the mules to the shambling buggy (his own property) which he drew from behind the stable, and steered for the " big road " and Sixth Mt. Zion Church. His deserted charges were gorging themselves.

I had been down the road the Negro took. Its sandy ruts curved away under branches hung with gray moss. It passed white-columned mansions set back in ancient groves. Paint scaled from the porticoes, and weathered shutters had here and there sprung from their hinges. In the bare reaches of country the huts of squatters, " sand-hillers," some-

[1] April, 1925.

times roofed with tin signs, lay in patches of brown cotton stalks. The way led beyond to the railroad depot, around which, for a mile in every direction, stretched the several thousand acres of one great planter. Here was his commissary, where tenants through the year came for store goods on credit, and when the crop was in, found, as likely as not, that they owed a balance to their landlord in cash. The account must then be carried over to the next year, and so seed and fertilizer must be bought through the creditor, and he must be given a lien on the cotton the tenants promised to raise.

Miles beyond the railroad, in the deep, deep country, nestled what was left of the old town which was the centre of life for the departed gentry of the district. Surviving affluence and tradition sufficed only to maintain the lovely Episcopal church with its wistaria-hung rectory. This village had once been selected for the capital of South Carolina, but its dances, its horse-racings, its politics, were things long ago forgotten.

Peg did not come back from " darkey meetin' " until the mules were rolling on the ground in agony from too much green grass—not a rib was to be seen in their swollen sides. Once arrived, he took the scene as a matter of course, and flung himself on an animal's head as we forced bottles of " dope " through grinding teeth and scrubbed a rough back with turpentine.

I left the heaving barn-yard to stroll across the fields to a little private cemetery whose funereal cedars I had spied from my window. It had long been abandoned. The encircling brick wall was crumbling in places. Weeds and briers had crowded out ivy and roses. In a prominent spot stood the high tomb of George McDuffie, one of the greatest South Carolinians before the Civil War. The boldly-cut name was almost obscured by the tangle of growth; the mortar had fallen from the stones, and lay where it had dropped.

In contrast, another grave in South Carolina came to mind—that of William Gregg, a Charleston merchant who revolted from the régime that McDuffie stood for. Gregg, as early as the 'forties, deplored slavery, planted peach orchards as against a one-crop system, and pleaded for good roads. He looked with compassion upon the Poor Whites, ousted by Negro chattels. He visited New England cities, laughed at McDuffie's belief that mills could not succeed in the South, and built the Graniteville cotton factory to prove the faith that was in him. Here he welcomed stranded white tenants and beaten farmers who had been driven into the hill country. He gave them work and wages, homes and school and church. He was the South's prophet of a new day.

Gregg was right, and McDuffie was wrong. Gregg's granite factories, environed now by thousands upon thousands of augmenting spindles, are sufficient tribute to his memory. McDuffie's sand hills lapse deeper into their languor.

Much of the McDuffie tradition survives in the Gregg achievement. It is this infusion of the old with the new which forced the Supreme Court to vexed decision in the outstanding matter of child labor, and which, in the South's opposition to the Child Labor Amendment, helped to balk the progress of federal legislation. Thus do ghosts of the long past rise up to plague us! What is the situation in the cotton manufacture of the South to-day that has been produced by this mixture of planter habit with industrial inspiration; and how does all this bear upon the prospect of New England's mills and upon the social conscience of the country?

Mention Southern cotton mills and the average American, if he thinks at all, thinks of child labor, and enters upon a round abuse of the tyrannous practice. The whole question has been clothed in lurid descriptions. Savage charges from the North have brought back fierce denials from the South; fact findings have been forgotten in the fury of controversy; assaults and defenses have become part and parcel of theories of government, so that strict-constructionist and federalist meet in the arena.

Though all this seems to be in keeping with the time-honored method of democratic progress, it is none the less stupidly superficial. The issue will be determined by causes underlying, and these causes may be perceived only in historical retrospect.

Frederick Law Olmsted avoided the heat of the slavery quarrel and, after open-minded inquiry, showed that the fever of absolute rights should be cooled down to the balancing of comparative expediencies; men rushed on to civil war in spite of him, but all the problems which he discerned and which he wished to leave to modified economic evolution, remained for painful settlement after Appomattox. Slavery was dissipating itself at the very time it was most frantically defended. Similarly, child labor in Southern cotton mills, just now when State legislatures are being so marshalled for its maintenance, is well on the road to extinction. This may be readily seen in a review of the course of the Southern industry.

William Gregg was a generation ahead of his time. The South would not go with him, but had to wallow deeper in the mire of slavery. Then came the Civil War, and spoliation and grief; but not awakening to repentance. The crude wrongs of Reconstruction kept Southern indignation and the spirit of revenge aflame. The insulted section would seek what redress it could through electing a Democratic President. Energies that did not go to protecting hearth and commonwealth were devoted to this project. In 1876 Tilden was counted out. The South felt itself outraged afresh. The year 1880 brought redoubled effort, this time to elect Hancock as against Garfield. Again Southern hopes were crushed.

Fury soon wore itself out, and a sudden change came over the South. It opened its eyes to see that abortive political reconstruction being over, real economic reconstruction must begin. This determination—humble, yet dignified, honest, and generous—had its birth and its fulfilment within the South. The program was, in short, to go to work in wholesome production with free labor, to be national instead of sectional, to mix manufacturing with agriculture. "We need fewer stump speakers and more stump pullers," was the cry to which thinking men rallied. Specie payments had been resumed. Prosperity overtook the depression that followed the crisis of 1873.

To manufacture cotton within the South was the obvious project. "Here is water, what hindereth?" Why should the South send its great staple to old or New England, accepting a pittance for the raw material as compared with the profits accruing from its manufacture? Gregg's philosophy was revived. The Poor Whites, jostled aside by slavery, were more than ever destitute, and a prime object in the building of mills was to give them employment.

Local communities squeezed out their last available nickels, elected the leading citizen—doctor, lawyer, merchant, preacher, or planter, it made no difference—president of the new manufacturing company, and sent him North to seek supplementary aid. Commission merchants, usually in return for agency for the mill's product, lent working capital, and textile machinery makers took stock in payment for equipment. Not that the North was wholly sympathetic or co-operative. Men like Edward Atkinson did their clever and persistent best to prove to the South that it could not succeed in its venture. New England cotton manufacturers, speaking in superior assurance or in jealous fear, declared that Southern labor was too unskilled and ill-adapted to industrial employment to succeed. Water-powers, it was granted, the South possessed, but of what advantage were these without a spinning climate such as that of New England? The South was remote from markets. Streams in the South were not clear enough for bleaching and dyeing purposes. The capital that had been raised in the South so promptly was a mere flash in the pan—it would soon be used up, and there were no more resources to be commandeered.

But the South, with pluck and luck, blasted one of these fallacies after another. Labor learned, artificial humidifiers made the cotton run smoothly in manufacture, a home market was exploited, unprecedentedly high profits went back into plant.

Nobody objected to the long hours, the low pay, or the working of women and children. It was a blessing to be able to earn bread. The mill villages were, as Gregg had put it earlier, " asylums for widows and orphans," and there were enough of these dependents in the post-war South. The mills, whether built in town or country, generally had to supply houses for their swarms of operatives. Besides these, in rural districts they had to build stores and churches and, as soon as possible, schools. The workers brought nothing but their necessity.

The projectors of the mills were in most cases the leaders the South had been accustomed to follow. They were often ex-Confederate officers. With their new inspiration went, of course, many characteristics which were hold-overs from the past. Their tradition was that of aristocrats, planters, slave-owners, States' Rights men, and, in the better sense, politicians. They were accustomed to assume leadership and accept responsibility. As their factories prospered, owners, partly through altruism and partly to prevent operatives from shifting from mill to mill, added to the attractiveness of their villages, joining recreational to educational and religious facilities. As competition for work yielded gradually to competition for workers, this tendency was further accelerated, until to-day Southern cotton mills have the most completely developed welfare system of any great industry.

It was natural that mill managers who had begun by taking initiative when all around them were dependent, should fail, as time wore on, to leave enough to the independence of their villagers. Thus paternalism which for many years was generous at length became calculating. As the Poor Whites most readily attracted were absorbed into the mills, agents were sent to scour the tenant farms and mountain hollows for new recruits. Gradually the workers, viewing these efforts, began to realize, however dimly, that they had a slight advantage they might ply. They became restive, and developed a tendency to make demands, instead of simply giving thanks for favors. At first this disposition was shown only by individuals, but living in communities developed in these isolated country people something of a group consciousness.

When the United States entered the World War, there was a drawing off of labor to army, to cantonment construction, to munition factory. Cotton prices were high, and profit returned to farming. Without their asking it, operatives' wages were raised 10 per cent at a clip and often. For the first time, the workers really began to feel their importance and power. After the armistice, when reductions in wages threatened, they became more or less receptive to the idea, almost wholly novel in their ranks, of unionism.

Big strikes in Columbus, Georgia, and Charlotte, North Carolina, with lesser demonstrations at many other factory centres, though generally lost by the hastily-organized workers, gave alarm to mill managements. Storming through press and pulpit and platform, they used all the approved methods of breaking strikes and preventing unionism—exclusion of organizers from company-owned towns, incitement of public and private police, cutting off of store credit, intimidation of weaker workers. Generally their belief or contention was to deny that their protégés were ungrateful for benefactions—it was the " outside agitator " who had fomented strife. In the end they set about to kill with kindness this outrageous independence of their operatives, however engendered. More than ever before was spent on villages, nurses, kindergartners, schools, swimming pools, Boy Scouts, and Young Men's Christian Associations.

The movement for restrictions upon child labor was naturally slow in arriving. The mill population was needy. As children had worked on the farms, it was taken for granted that, when transferred to the mills, they would continue to be productive. Too often exploitation was the design of the parents, though they could hardly avoid the evil. Mill owners were the leading members of their communities, and counted heavily in State legislatures, where they organized powerful lobbies. If operatives voted, it was for demagogues who raised the issue of the Negro, never that of their own industrial rights. Moreover, were not the mills " doing everything for this element "? And finally, the South was poor, and must be encouraged, not hampered, in its struggle against the competition of Northern mills.

When, however, it was apparent that State legislation could no longer be staved off, an attempt was made to turn defeat into victory by pleading that local regulation was effective and should not be superseded by federal interference. Investigators sent by the national government were declared to be prying sentimentalists, all from the North. Congressional debates were inspired by New England cotton manufacturers jealous of Southern progress and anxious to have the South's advantage in child labor taken away.

The cotton manufacture in Great Britain, New England, and the South tells a story of repetition surprisingly complete and accurate. Consider the paternalistic company town. In Scotland there was Robert Owen's New Lanark, with almost every modern refinement of welfare work, from community kitchen to village band. In Massachusetts was Lowell, founded twenty years later with company church and school and boarding houses, lyceum and literary society. In the South two decades later still was Gregg's Graniteville, with benevolent proprietor supreme. Later came Piedmont and Pelzer, Clifton and a hundred others like them. The South has learned nothing from this history. England and New England, except in rare instances, have abandoned company town and paternalism—mills moved to cities, alien operatives preferred racial seclusion. Identical results will follow in the South—factory villages will be incorporated into the towns they encircle, and managements will pay in taxes what they now spend directly in welfare facilities. Already there are mill agents which knew not Joseph.

In the matter of child labor, New England mills went blindly ahead opposing regulation, and legislatures temporized, entirely oblivious of the success of the Ten Hours Movement in the Mother Country as championed by Oastler and Ashley. Every possible argument pro and con, from the sanctity of *laissez faire* to the effect of shortened hours upon production—was thrashed out upon Boston's Beacon Hill as it had been in Westminster Hall. Yet the South has remained historically unconscious. Reports of congressional hearings in 1916 on the first national child labor Act (largely involving the Southern cotton manufacture) repeat almost word for word the questions and answers in the English Blue Book of 1816. Southern legislatures have rejected the Child Labor Amendment in the same phrases as were unavailingly used in Lancashire and Massachusetts.

Or take trade unionism. British operatives, probably during the Industrial Revolution more put upon than Anglo-Saxon people have ever been before or since, and without political suffrage or the first shadow of industrial cohesion, have since sent the one-time secretary of their powerful union to be minister of labor in a labor government. In New England cotton mills unionism has made slower progress; while some mill cities are almost completely organized, others have small union membership. But the union protest is perfectly understood, and the right to organize is everywhere allowed. Trade unionism in the South, rendered especially tardy by the number of Negroes in the working population generally, and by the heavy proportion of women and children in the cotton mills, is a shocking concept to employers and, in the main, a vast mystery to operatives. In most places, managements have taken paternalism to be a sufficient guard against the invader. Where this has not worked, direct suppression has been used. This failing, some mills have progressed along the regular course to company unionism. This in turn is proving a fair-weather craft—suitable enough in the plain sailing over the ripples of sanitary drinking fountains, but not fit for the squalls of wage demands.

The obstructionism of the Southern cotton manufacture is explained by its adolescence. It is in process of maturing. New England has some time since caught up with old England in product, in markets, in perfection of selling organization, in expensiveness of power. It has passed England in wages and conditions of work. The South commenced with many differential advantages as compared with New England—abundance of power, cheapness of construction, nearness to raw cotton, plentifulness and subservience of intelligent labor, length of hours, and lowness of wages. Most of these differentials are on the way towards disappearance, due to the very success of the industry in the South and total economic advance of the section. Mills manufacture finer goods than can be made from their local cotton; in producing for a national instead of for a regional market, distance from New York as a selling point becomes a problem; legislatures have diminished hours and raised age limits for children.

Yet the labor factor remains the chief advantage for the South; and it proposes to hold to this. Trade unions, incorporation of company-owned villages, and the Child Labor Amendment are alike opposed in the effort to preserve a sectional asset. We are witnessing a grand review of all the arguments that have ever been employed to bolster industrial backwardness and autocratic power.

But this is perhaps the last time these staunch supports, so long in the service of the cotton trade, will be set up by manufacturers to be bowled over by public opinion. If what has been a sectional asset now threatens, through Southern opposition to the Child Labor Amendment, to become a national liability, the danger cannot last. The Amendment has indeed been lost, but what legislative fiat was not for the present able to compel, economic development will undoubtedly, a little later, assure. Why is this true?

In the making of competitive cloths the New England mill is doomed. The Southern manufacturer enjoys a comparative advantage that averages about 15 per cent. The New England mill in competition with the Southern mill is " marginal "—that is, it must be content with a smaller profit in good times, and must reduce operations or close down altogether when depression overtakes the industry. There are agents and superintendents in the non-cotton growing States who stupidly shut their eyes to the facts. There are others who, with sufficient dread of the real situation, keep up an optimism by relying upon the well-established character of their manufacture and by reminding themselves of the traditional ingenuity of the Yankee in cutting corners. Still others, with disappearing profits in the last two years, have pressed their labor harder, only to find the workers rebelling. Finally, there is the large number of manufacturers, many of them presiding over the oldest and greatest establishments north of Mason and Dixon's line, who acknowledge defeat in the North and seek salvation by moving South.

In the last 11 months of 1923, a New England authority estimates, the spindles in place in the South increased by 518,000, while in the non-cotton growing States they decreased by 107,000. Massachusetts alone lost 35,000 spindles. The tide has turned. The old attitude towards the South has changed. It is not pretended that many New England manufactories will bodily move South. Geographical shifts in a great industry come less obviously, but no less certainly. What happens is that a Lowell or a Lawrence company in contemplating extensions looks only to the South. Or a visitor goes down an impressive alley of mills lining a century-old canal; though yard-men are about, and here and there a building vibrates with machinery, the leaves that have fallen from the elms and litter the vacant street seem somehow symbolic. Cloth that costs 34 cents per pound to manufacture here, costs the same company, in its Southern factory, only 22 cents. One mill makes as much as the other loses, and so the disadvantaged New England establishment continues to live on sufferance. But further along one comes to a great structure that is utterly silent. This plant has earned its capitalization several times over in better years, and now will never open as a cotton mill again.

As the cotton industry augments in the South, the South's differential advantage will be eaten into. Increased demand for Southern sites and labor and cotton and power will raise manufacturing costs in the favored section. The newcomers will not invest so largely in paternalism as have their neighbors, the Southern mill men. They will look upon the native white population, accustomed to a low standard of living and untainted by "radical proclivities" or foreign blood, as an exploitable factor in the industrial calculus. The responsibility of the managers will be to themselves, and not, in the old Southern sincerity or the new Southern pretense, to the operatives. Gradually welfare work everywhere in the South will shrink, because in the new competition that will invest the Southern section, every dollar must be rendered immediately productive. Also, with increased wages and bettered standards of living, Southern operatives will demand money in their pay envelopes instead of seeing it spent in all sorts of social services. Trade unionism will strengthen its foothold in the South. As the industry is more and more concentrated in this section, labor organization, indeed, may become more nearly complete than it has been in the North, for there will no longer be a definitely non-union field to which the manufacturer may, as at present, transfer operations when pressed by his workers.

The South is now on a one-manufacture system as much as on a one-crop system. The worker's chances to assert himself are limited so long as there is only the cotton mill for him to go to. As it is at present, cotton mill wages cannot rise much above income on the land. But as more mills are built in the South, other branches of the industry besides spinning and weaving will be entered upon. Finishing plants will increase in numbers, and more machine shops will be set up. The supplying of power will grow in importance, and all the institutions of credit will expand, quickening industrial facilities all along the line. With alternate employments open to Southern workers, the cotton mill will have to offer higher and higher standards of remuneration, for it is agreed that little fresh labor remains to be conducted into factory employment, even under present conditions.

Hours of work permitted in cotton manufacturing will be shortened in the South as they have been in the North by State legislative enactment, whether to justify opposition to national interference, or whether in response to a more powerful and independent labor vote. Moreover, the unions will bend every effort towards shorter hours, and cotton mill managements will thus be influenced directly and through the necessity of meeting competition of other industries. And unionism will effectively oppose child labor, to protect standards of adults if not to prove humanity.

In a word, the cotton manufacturing South will lose its peculiarity. It will come to national standards. As the great seat of the industry, it will be responsible to the national conscience, no longer pleading, on grounds of sectional patriotism, for the leniency of a costly subsidy in exploited workers.

Looking forward to these developments, which every indication foretells, the Southern cotton manufacturing industry has two choices. It may by opposing right standards deny its old altruism, and fly in the face of the inevitable. Or it may accept the terms of progress and celebrate its best traditions.

4. Some Southern Industrialists [1]

Falling Creek where it enters the James River seven miles below Richmond, Virginia, is "a place of old emprise." Here the London Company, in 1620, promoted iron works. It would seem from the number of men engaged in the erection and the length of time they were about it that a blast furnace, a finery and a chafery were designed. John Berkeley and his men "made Proof of good Iron Oar, and brought the whole Work so near Perfection, that they writ

[1] January, 1929.

Word to the Company in *London*, that they did not doubt but to finish the Work, and have plentiful Provision of Iron for them by the next *Easter*." However, the massacre of March, 1622, put an end to the project; the Indians " fell so hard upon this . . . Place, that no Soul was saved, but a Boy and a Girl who, with great Difficulty, hid themselves."

At intervals of generations desultory attempts were made at revival of the works, but Falling Creek remained a wilderness. The very site of the original enterprise was covered by washings from the adjacent bank. The ore bogs were forgotten, and a nearby supply of lead was lost sight of, rediscovered and lost again. The lands of the vicinity were cropped out with 300 years of a wasteful agriculture. The year 1928 found the spot as desolate and silent as when the English colonists first ventured there.

Now, suddenly, all is changed. A ten-million dollar plant is being erected there for the manufacture of rayon by the viscose process. The annual output will be more than three million pounds, and upwards of two thousand workers will be employed. This is just another evidence of the South's industrial awakening from a long sleep.

Our Industrial Revolution in the South has been as precipitate and spectacular as that in England earlier. As in the old country, we have been slow to recognize the change, slower in analyzing its consequences in the present, and tardiest of all in conjecturing what will fall out in the future. We are still in the fever heat of it, and possess no perspective. There is perhaps no single social alteration so potent in its concomitants as the widespread introduction of manufactures in a hitherto agricultural economy, unless it be possibly the abolition of a system of slavery. We are now beginning to be interested in the figures who instituted this new adventure. We scarcely know their names, let alone their thoughts, their acts, their certain significance in the pell-mell of progress.

Industrial advance in the South came first, prominently, in the cotton manufacture. The lives of the vast majority of the important enterprisers remain unwritten. A few of them left record of their thoughts in books and pamphlets, and more in speeches and reports that found their way into newspapers of the day. But in the main it is necessary to inquire in the old localities of those who knew them—their former operatives, superintendents, shareholders and business competitors. Such a search provokes a rich response of incident and anecdote, out of which a student acquainted with the march of the development may form a picture, with many allowances for error, of the place each man occupied in the evolution. It is difficult to choose types, for all were apt to overlap with the rest, and in the sketches of significant figures that follow I am aware of over-simplification.

The most interesting apostle of industrialism in the South before the Civil War was William Gregg of South Carolina. He was the one swallow that did not make a summer. He represents the link with the legitimate period of Southern industry, if I may use that term. His advocacy owed much to the fact that when an orphan of twelve years or so he was introduced to the cotton manufacture by his uncle, Jacob Gregg, who built a small factory in Georgia. This was the period of stimulation of American manufactures incident to the War of 1812. William probably had a good start on his apprenticeship in the mill when the enterprise, with many others, was ruined by the flood of British goods which entered this country after the peace. But the boy's education in the manual arts did not cease, for, his uncle having been a watchmaker and jeweler, he was put to learning these handicrafts.

When he had accumulated a fortune and temporarily retired from business in the 'thirties, he luckily ran across the little Vaucluse cotton factory in the upper part of South Carolina. This mill had been built by George McDuffie and others who favored nullification and wanted to show that the South could supply its own manufactures. It was in a declining way. Gregg was persuaded that if the founders had put as much energy into industrial management as they put into preaching political revolt, the mill would have succeeded. Futhermore— and this was the sovereign stroke of his thought—if the South cultivated industry and so approximated its economic pursuits to those of the North, political differences, particularly on the score of the protective tariff, would disappear. Thus to his interest in manufactures, born in an older period of national patriotism, was added a philosophy of industry very pertinent to a later day of economic degeneration in the South.

Gregg put the Vaucluse mill on its feet, but did not buy it. This might have been the limit of his services had he not, in the late 'thirties, moved to Charleston. Here he found two main elements in the public life: planters or men dependent upon the planting interest seething with political animosity against the North, and an economically more active group of commercial men who invested their surplus funds at low interest in bank stock or public securities. This was a combination ready to his hand. He was stirred to new enterprise. Having visited the textile districts of the North, he published a series of articles in the Charleston Courier in 1844-5, in which he read sermons to both the elements in his audience. To the planter dissenters he declared that their political idols could never answer the prayer for economic plenitude—that exclusive devotion to agriculture must be the ruin of any people. To the rich merchants he argued that their future lay not in forwarding impracticable projects of linking their port with the Ohio valley by railroads built with State subsidies, but rather in developing South Carolina by investment of their relatively idle funds in industrial enterprise. Their promised land lay not beyond the Appalachians, but at home. He wanted farms to be balanced by factories, and they would be if Charleston traders, instead of scowling at their desolate back country while they cast bright glances upon Cincinnati, would join with him to initiate cotton manufacturing.

Be it said to Charleston's credit, the city listened to Gregg with a degree of enthusiasm, and within a short time a third of a million dollars was subscribed for a large cotton factory in the up-country. All of Gregg's bold effort was needed to persuade the legislature to grant a charter, but once the Graniteville factory was under way, in 1848, it promptly began to justify his predictions. Others followed his lead here and there throughout the South, though their mills met with indifferent success in operation. Graniteville continued to be an oasis.

About the mill Gregg built a tasteful village in which the Poor Whites of the district, who were the special object of his solicitude, found asylum. Here instead of the old illiteracy on the land they found a day school for all children up to 12, upon which attendance was compulsory, and night classes for adults. The workers were paid cash wages, low and for long hours it is true, but marking a grateful release from the vassalage of the credit system in the country. He knew that he was dealing with people in their economic infancy, and he was not afraid to play the despot. Graniteville was a temperance town. He contrived not to limit their self-respect, but to increase it.

Gregg had antecedents in the South in village welfare work and doubtless in his philosophy of manufactures as well, but his thought was so clear, his voice so resonant, his achievement so brilliant that others must shine in his reflection. Graniteville prospered in panic and depression and weathered the war, to be completely refitted before Gregg's death in 1867 for a new course of accomplishment. But for the section as a whole, the war was the end of an epoch in manufactures in the South. Gregg had essayed the impossible, and had succeeded for himself and his immediate locality only. Reliance upon the black hand on the hoe had been victorious over espousal of the white hand transferred to the spindle. The onrush toward civil war was not to be gainsaid. Graniteville and its concomitants were the swan song of the first South of industry mixed with agriculture.

The war left time and money for only the immediates. Every man was for himself. What collective effort there was took form in bitter insurgency against the Reconstruction. Economic convalescence required 15 years before, about 1880, there was an outburst of industrial upbuilding. But in the interval of collapse two men demand notice. They were both of South Carolina, H. P. Hammett and F. W. Dawson.

Hammett was much like Gregg, whom he knew and by whom he must have been influenced. In his personal history, his arguments for manufactures, the management of his mill and in his courage he more nearly resembled the master of Graniteville than any other Southern industrial enterpriser known to me. He was born in Greenville County in 1822. He derived from Samuel Slater, " the father of American manufactures," for he learned the business from William Bates, who had worked in the celebrated little Pawtucket factory. In 1819 Bates, an orphan boy, walked from Rhode Island to seek his fortune in the South. After working in several tiny mills in North and South Carolina, he bought a water power site on Rocky Creek near Greenville and built a wooden mill of hardly more than 1000 spindles, the yarn being bartered in " bunches," by wagon, all the way over into Tennessee.

Hammett picked up what education he could in a country school and began teaching, clerking in a store at Hamburg in vacations. He drifted to the school at Batesville, married the eldest daughter of William Bates, and was taken into partnership in the mill, having charge of the office work. He remained at Batesville fifteen years, until the mill was sold in 1862. He purchased Garrison Shoals on the Saluda River, but did not utilize the site for a decade, for he entered the army, being detailed for duty in the Confederate tax office. In 1866 he became president of the run-down Greenville and Columbia Railroad, which he much improved.

Resigning from the railroad in 1870, he determined to build a great cotton mill. There was a little grist mill at the Shoals, with just one log to throw the water to the Greenville side of the stream. The spot was desolate. It required imagination and hardihood to foresee a great industry there, and to conjure the means of its construction out of the beaten South. In April of 1873 the Piedmont Company was organized, with $75,000 capital subscribed from Greenville and Charleston. The following February a charter was obtained and the capital fixed at $200,000, some being taken by a Northern machinery maker. Scarcely had construction commenced when the panic of 1873 crushed the enterprise. Subscribers refused to pay their instalments, or sold out at what they could get for their stock. But Hammett was indomitable. In 1875 building was resumed, the workers being paid not in money but in grocery orders for which Hammett pledged his personal credit. In March of the following year the machinery was started—5000 spindles and 112 looms.

A principal idea of Hammett in building the mill was to make it of service to the Poor Whites of the region. They poured in as soon as the village was up. Two large families, the Grovers and Thackers from the neighborhood of the old Saluda factory, were almost sufficient in themselves for running the looms. Hammett will be longest remembered for his wise paternalism at Piedmont. His village became the pattern from which scores of others copied. He insisted on making the community decent and orderly. Mountain wagons would come into the town peddling corn whiskey at five cents for a tin cup full. These Hammett drove out; drunkenness was cause for dismissal from employment. His physical stature assisted his discipline. He was so large that he had a special buggy constructed for his use. He was dignified and generally wore a silk hat and Prince Albert coat. He spoke little and always with deliberation. Though his grandchildren, brought to see him on Sunday afternoons, remember him as stern, his workers of every station came to him freely. When in his last illness he talked to one of his superintendents about the Piedmont villagers he wept like a child, and refused to be led away from the subject.

The first mill was more than doubled in capacity and two others were built before his death, making Piedmont, with almost 50,000 spindles and 1300 looms, one of the great cotton mills of the world, and particularly well known in the China trade for its three-yard sheetings. Piedmont was the nursery of the Industrial Revolution in the South. In a quarter of a century it sent out 40 superintendents to manage half a million spindles.

The Industrial Revolution in the South, as in England, passed through several stages. It was born without attracting much notice, was discountenanced, grew despite disapproval, was recognized and earnestly espoused, was glorified, and lastly was modified. F. W. Dawson is a good representative of the period of recognition and advocacy. He had an advantage over some others mentioned in this paper in that, being a foreigner, he possessed a detachment from the scene about him. Dawson was born and educated in London, wrote for the stage, and read history. With the fall of Sumter his ardent, romantic nature led him to enlist on the Confederate cruiser Nashville at Southampton in November, 1861. In June of the next year, desiring more active service in the Southern cause, he transferred, as a private, to Purcell's Battery, Hill's Division, Army of Northern Virginia. Promoted for valiant action at Mechanicsville, May of 1864 found him a captain and ordnance officer of Fitzhugh Lee's Division. He was three times wounded, and imprisoned at Fort Delaware.

After the surrender, he had only a three-cent postage stamp in his uniform. He weathered a succession of failures and drifted into newspapering in Richmond, shifting in 1866 to the Charleston Mercury. In 1873 he was editor and part owner of the combined News and Courier. He was a large, athletic, handsome man, imperious and sudden, tenderhearted and generous, and above all devoted to the social recovery of the South. He applied the lesson of England's progress to the stricken Southern States—he preached industrialism, crop diversification, immigration of agricultural workers from Europe and artisans from the North. When a new factory in the South came to his notice he dramatized the news for the public. More than anyone else he was the apostle who cried up the " cotton mill campaign " which resulted in a boom for spinning the staple at home. He pictured the true economic reconstruction, vivid and pulsing. Henry W. Grady worked much to the same purpose, but he splashed color on his canvas, Turnerlike; Dawson on the other hand etched his picture in distinct, incisive lines, and he won not passing applause, but a loyal, growing, instructed following.

Dawson led the fight against duelling in South Carolina, and was honored for it by the Pope. A wretched fate overtook him, more than ordinarily unforgivable because he was so fair and courageous. He was shot down in cold blood for resenting an affront to a Swiss girl who was governess to his children.

A young Southerner went North in the early 'eighties to buy machinery for another man's cotton mill. " Where are you from? " he was asked. " Pinnook," he answered. " Pinnook? What the devil kind of a name is that for a place? " If George A. Gray's pronunciation had been more exact, he would have made it clear that his home town in North Carolina was called Pinhook, but that probably would not have helped any. His father, a Mecklenburg County farmer, died suddenly, leaving a wife and seven children. George, the youngest, worked in the Pinhook cotton factory of Caleb Lineberger near what is now Gastonia, at the age of 10 earning 10 cents a day. Soon after he started to work, his arm was broken in three places in a pulley. Narrowly escaping an amputation, he was eight months in getting well. The proprietor of the factory persuaded him to go to the country school during convalescence, and this was his only formal education.

The Pinhook factory is reduced now to ruined foundations overgrown with vines; the little wooden dam on the south fork of the Catawba is long since washed away; the village of plank shanties has been dismantled. And yet in the great trees and the lawn grass that has successfully contended against the weeds all these years, there is about the spot the indubitable memory of long habitation that clings to the most neglected of such places. Some day it will be remembered only because George Gray came from there. He got to be superintendent of the factory, and used to cut ice from the old breast wheel to make a day's run in the mill. He loved machinery, and learned every minutest trifle in its skilful operation. He was engaged to equip and start other, modern, mills. He saved his money. When he was 19 he had never received more than 75 cents a day, yet he had accumulated some hundreds of dollars.

In 1888 he started his own mill at the junction of two railroads in Gaston County. The place had only a dozen families, but he predicted a great future for it in cotton manufacturing. Others have contributed importantly to the result which he foretold, but he was the father of the development. Now Gaston County must be mentioned in the same breath with the Manchester and New Bedford districts. Its hundred mills with more than a million producing spindles turn out annually goods worth over $50,000,000.

Gray was a dynamo of nervous energy. Touch him, and sparks came off. He lived his life on tiptoes. An objective once in his mind, he drove at it incessantly. He went to his mills at 5:30 on summer mornings, and at 6 o'clock in winter, and was the last man to leave. He had a passion for economical contrivance. Condemning the old awkward poor work at little Pinhook, he insisted on installing the latest improvements in every plant under his care. He is said to have been the first man to run an electrically driven mill in the South. At their very outset he welcomed the development of hydro-electric stations. At his death he was president of 16 mills, and he visited every one every day. His ear was so attuned that if something was amiss in a remote corner of a great room resounding with machinery, he would detect it. His foremost contribution to the Industrial Revolution in the South was that of technical proficiency.

Gray regimented his life—his rising and retiring were on the dot, he drank water at certain times during the day, if he said " wait two minutes " he meant exactly that. But his eye twinkled, and people liked to call him by his first name. He insisted upon having associates he could rely upon. He used to say of his Negro stable man, befriended after his hand had been cut off in a saw mill, that he would be willing to convert all he had into cash and put the money with Joe with instructions to keep it, and he believed not a penny would be missing after 20 years. That was no greater tribute to Joe than to his employer.

Thus far I have spoken of Gregg, who first woke the public mind to industry; Hammett, who ventured upon factory building in the darkest days of Reconstruction; Dawson, the publicist who popularized the experiment in economic diversification; and Gray, the expert technician who helped make every former hope reality. These borrowed in experience and spirit from the Old South or from the industrial background of England. The last figure in my gallery, D. A. Tompkins, belongs distinctly to the post-war South. While his career rounded up the advocacies of his predecessors, he represents the emergence in Southern industry of a new type, the engineer.

Ten years old at the outbreak of the Civil War, Tompkins was familiar with the routine of a large South Carolina cotton plantation, and afterwards came to understand the limitations of this agricultural system. After two years in the State university he decided that the South of his day would need fewer men of literary culture than of mechanical proficiency, so he transferred to a technical school in the

North. A long apprenticeship in the iron industry followed, with erection of plants in Germany. He did not forget his belief in the possibilities of the South, and in 1882 established himself in Charlotte, North Carolina, in a tiny shop as "engineer, machinist, and contractor." He was among the first trained men in Southern industry—trained not only in mechanical skill, but in the faculty of social analysis. He began with small repair jobs—threading pipes for steam laundries, mending cotton gins. He got the agency for an engine, and proved himself an able salesman. His business grew. He was a promoter. He would single out an alert man in a nearby town, get to know him, and propose that the community needed a cotton mill to increase the value of its raw material. A meeting of citizens would be convinced by Tompkins not only of the value of his project, but of its practicability through instalment payments on locally subscribed shares. He would design and erect the factory and persuade machinery makers to take payment in stock.

He was probably directly responsible for the building of more cotton mills than any other one man. He organized and built within a few months a chain of efficient cotton seed oil mills. As gifted as any one who had gone before him in bold conception, he was better equipped than his predecessors in capacity for thorough execution of his plans on a broad scale. He was in no sense local. His patriotism was that of an American. He insisted that the

South, through industry, must take its place in the life of the nation. As an industrialist he shook off old sectional prejudices, and ardently espoused the protective tariff. He thought in economic terms. He foresaw and forwarded a self-contained textile industry in the South, with varied products, means for their finishing, and the manufacture as well as the repair of mill machinery.

Tompkins' career may be taken as closing the long period of argument for manufactures and the setting up of a physical plant to carry plans into execution. Since have come two other stages in the evolution—the glorification of the industry, in which profit has been set forth in the guise of patriotism, and the answer to this in attempts to curb capitalism in protection of labor and preservation of social rights. The figures in these later periods have only defined an inevitable quarrel. The members of the older company, instead of apportioning benefits, created out of hand the means for Southern progress.

5. Three Southerners [1]

It is not often that an individual, in however long a life, compasses, in its emergence, development and fulfilment, an entire social epoch. Robert Owen was one of these. During his nearly 90 years the domestic system of manufactures was swallowed into the maw of the Industrial Revolution, mercantilism

[1] July, 1922.

gave way before the strident self-sufficiency of Manchester optimists, and the claims of these were in turn refuted by the early Utopians, the ill-starred Chartists, the philanthropists of the Factory Acts, the little circle of Christian Socialists and, last, the solemn savagery of "Das Kapital." The draper's apprentice lived to know Karl Marx.

If this is rare, how much rarer for one to be able, at a point of time, to talk with those who represent the several successive phases of a long development. Lately, in a trip through the South undertaken to discover how the section sprang from agriculture, slavery and separatism into manufacturing, wage labor and national participation, I met (in three days) three men who, each in his distinctive way, make up the whole story. Thus I had the Southern Industrial Revolution, from first to last, in a focus. The panorama was uncannily contracted, as when one looks through the wrong end of a telescope.

I

In a shoddy little city which gives no hint of the importance that lies in the buzzing mills that encircle it, I was told to go first to see Colonel M———. His home was a dingy, rambling frame building. A dusty vine looped itself about the porch pillars and cast shadows through the open door into the hall. I clanged the bell and stood looking at the bare, unwashed floor, the rigid old sofa and a smoked kerosene lamp on a tilting table. After long waiting and more jangling of the bell, an old colored woman came shuffling out from the back to tell me that the Colonel was away, but that if I would come through the house, " Jeems " would direct me to him. The back yard was weed-grown to the kitchen windows; two old brick servants' houses stood away from the dwelling, and between these an ancient darkey was sawing firewood.

" You don' know whar de Cunl's office at? " he asked in genuine astonishment. " Why, de Cunl's office, hit's cross fum de cote house whar got de clock in de tower."

The second-floor room in " lawyers' row " was like many another Southern attorney's den, and yet was peculiar to its occupant. The air was gray with stale tobacco smoke, the drab walls were fly-specked, the furniture, upholstered in worn horse-hair, was piled with dirty papers. A load of yellowing sheets had accumulated on a center table, and this pile was surmounted by a topless panatelas box filled with granulated burley and a dozen clay pipes, their long curved stems in a jackstraw jumble. Summoned by my footfalls, the Colonel, the genius of the place, entered seemingly from nowhere. I could catalogue him at the first glance. He was of the old school, and could have been cast for the stage without the stroking of an eyelash. A Prince Albert coat, over-long, turning a bit greenish, and with silk-faced lapels, hung limp and loose about his tall frame. Imperious eyes looked at me from under tufted brows, his tobacco-stained moustache and goatee worked spasmodically, and when he lifted off his great flopping straw hat his hair was purest white.

I explained my errand and, not without some examination, was bowed to a seat and offered a pipe. " That's all stuff and nonsense about the war (to him there had been but one in the history of this world) making the Southern people change their way of life," he exploded. " We have always been business people around here from the first—manufactured in iron and wood and cotton. The war kind of broke us up, and we had it pretty hot during Reconstruction, but afterwards we just got back on the track."

In a front office the Colonel's nephew, clad in perfectly pressed Palm Beach and perched on his desk, interrupted us by telephoning to the station agent, between puffs at his cigarette, to deliver a crate of beer he had ordered.

I asked whether it was mountaineers who came down to supply hands for the cotton-mill renaissance of the 'eighties. The Colonel was indignant. " Magazine writers from the North tell you that!" In his excitement he commenced knocking the lit ashes out of his pipe, covering his knees with sparks, and immediately began refilling the bowl. " Magazine writers from the North, I say! The mill people came from right 'round here, and they weren't any paupers either. They'd been farmers before, and lots of 'em owned their land, too." Only the thudding tick-tock of a wall clock broke the old gentleman's satisfied silences. I could not disabuse his mind of the conviction that the South had never been brought to resolve upon a new policy when it had forgotten Calhoun in the lesson of Appomattox and despaired of political revenge through the tortured years of Radical Rule. As he has countenanced no improvements in his own dwelling or the property surrounding it, so he has clung affectionately and proudly to a social and economic system that is over, stoutly resolving not to recognize its decay.

II

The next town I visited is one of bitter memory. Near it, during the Civil War, was one of the worst of the prison camps, where men dug holes in the earth and, in their starvation and frenzy, were more degraded than wild beasts. The Confederacy, starving and frenzied itself, was powerless to prevent the wretchedness of its captives. Twenty years after the war the town had not roused itself. Its inaction and its poverty made a vicious circle. It sulked and nursed its rancor and despaired. It came to have no excuse for being.

The fairy story of its revival was told me by the president of the principal bank. A man of fifty-five, a strange mixture of vague dreaminess and keenness, he first answered me that he was a poor informant on the cotton manufacturing growth of the place. But I had been warned of his hesitancy, and when the local clearing house had adjourned from the director's room, he ushered me in. He leaned carelessly against the table while in an intense voice, as though the events were fresh upon him, he explained that in the late 'eighties a Presbyterian minister had come to the town to hold a " protracted meeting." The morbid introspection of the people lent itself to the evangelist's purposes. They flocked to the tabernacle from miles about. Disobeying ministerial traditions, the preacher analyzed the need as that of material improvement, a new social objective. The unemployed in the town and the pauperized Poor Whites of the district needed means of support. He hit upon cotton mills as the cure. He related moral woes to physical depletions. All the people needed to pull together in a common cause. He fired them to a new purpose, so that the town tingled with his strictures and took hope at his encouragements.

A mass meeting of citizens was held in a warehouse, was opened by prayer, and subscriptions were taken toward the establishment of a cotton factory which would initiate activity. Three ministers took prominent part in the organization, and their helpers were pillars of the local churches. The amount contemplated was over-subscribed. The mill thus founded took the name of the town and has been more than ordinarily successful from the outset. It has never had a company store, never permitted night work, never employed any but the " home people " for whom it was inaugurated, and almost no shares have been held outside the immediate community. Other companies followed, and as mills increased saloons disappeared, streets were paved, better homes were built, and wealth was more evenly distributed.

My informant brought from the safe an old leather-bound ledger in which the minutes of the organization meetings were taken down in the not very clerkly hand of the preacher-promoter. As he read aloud over my shoulder I could feel that he was only sorry for the social plan of the Old South from which he and his friends had emerged young enough to help make the New South. The conversion to manufactures had broken suddenly and powerfully upon them; the religion of industry had been a psychical experience. The Old South, he understood, had given to the New South only a sense of obligation and an idealism which, tutored in a better school, had worked a blessed miracle.

III

I reached my next town in a long downpour of rain that had soaked the muddy streets, stained the cheap clap-board houses, and brought with it a wet mantle of soot from the palisading factory chimneys. In spirits none too good anyway, I received a damp welcome in an up-to-date mill office on the main street. The fingers of a brisk little stenographer were twinkling over her keys. I waited a half hour for the busy president, and finally almost forced my way in, to find him dictating in summary sentences while he chewed angrily on a dead cigar. A glance at my brief case persuaded him I had something to sell, so he had few words for me. When I explained that no dissertation could ever hope for purchasers he relented, and wanted to know what I was after. A thick-set man of forty, with a mass of very red hair in waves and mats, a face almost equally red and perspiring freely, his dress untidy, he snapped his brevities at me vigorously.

When he learned I could speak his language, he abruptly offered to run me in his roadster around the ring of mills that lay just beyond the town limits. He handled his battered, muddy little car ruthlessly, and kept nervously banging the windshield up and down to see whether the rain would come in. He was little disposed to rationalize the growth of cotton manufactures in the South, but dwelt upon immediate problems. He wanted a protective tariff, and cited differences in labor costs in England, France, Germany, and Japan to back his point. He was sure the ownership in the Southern industry was being concentrated; he himself had bought up most of the shares in his company, whether held by local investors or Northern commission firms and machinery makers. The South, he declared, is the inevitable location of the world cotton manufacture, but there was a hard-headed conservatism in his outlook too, and he thought the section would have to win out through a well-pursued business policy.

His mill was the last word in engineering achievement, with every provision for expansion, fire prevention, and transportation. He waved his hand proudly toward the glass sawtooth roof of the low weave sheds, and pointed out new devices he was experimenting with. I tried to get him back to the birth of the industry in the town, but he was scarcely interested in those struggles except as they had flowered in the achievement he was eager to show. He told me of a company that had started with $15,000 capital, receiving installments on shares of 50 cents a week and commencing operations in an old wood-working shop. As we came down to the railroad the sun burst from the clouds and the haze lifted. Steam arose from the shiny, sweating backs of mules as they churned about a platform at which cotton bales were being unloaded. My guide yanked the windshield down again and pointed across to a great factory with a contracted, antiquated central portion overgrown with ivy. The car jerked to a stop with a chattering of brakes. " You see that middle building? " he asked. And then with hearty admiration: " Well, that's the damn little mill that began it all! "

He was no more likely to guard the tradition of the ante-bellum South than he had experienced the birth pains of the economic reconstruction which signalized the 'eighties and 'nineties. Neither social oppositions to industry nor social compulsions toward it had meaning for him. The long error of the

South and its later resolve to make progress have bred up this new and practical type of manufacturer who does not count causes but plays for results, who knows his business and, with his American fellows everywhere, studies his chances, hardens his muscle, and exults in his fight.

6. Two Industrial Revolutions [1]

Students of American history, though they have had before them the suggestiveness of the English Industrial Revolution, have not sufficiently recognized that the Southern States, a century later than Britain, experienced an alteration in economic objective strikingly similar. Particularly, one cannot help lamenting with Mr. Sioussat (History Teacher's Magazine, September, 1916) that classes in Southern schools and colleges should be acquainted with what happened in Lancashire and the West Riding and remain largely unfamiliar with the facts and significance of industrial changes in the Carolinas and Georgia. The omission by tutors has shown a counterpart in the attitude of laymen. It is ironical that a movement toward manufactures which was consciously undertaken and pursued with deliberate social purpose has not been viewed in its analogies to the past. The rise of the factory system in England and later in the Northern States did not prompt the South, in many practicable cases, to anticipate

[1] October, 1921.

demonstrated errors or to take maximum advantage of her opportunities. Not to mention less pressing phases, the old tortured history of cautions thrown about child labor meant nothing to us. Oastler and Shaftesbury never lived.

This paper means to remind of salient comparisons between the English original and the Southern manifestation, with the hope that others may interest themselves productively in the subject. It is not too late to profit. White Southern fields that a hundred years ago had a far alliance with black British cities of which Dickens' " Coketown " is the picture, now have the nearer tie with smoking stacks of their own, and more and more will be rising. The English Industrial Revolution was four decades along before the effort to have the strange giant serve instead of hindering society was articulate. Our 40-year giant is just beginning to stretch himself and feel his strength.

Both revolutions came suddenly and proceeded rapidly. In each instance textiles were the first affected by the new methods; in each spinning took the lead over weaving—in England because there was a wait upon invention, in the South for lack of experience, from the presence of abundant raw material and a ready demand in older industrial districts for a partial product. In England textiles promptly conducted to other manufactures; though this is occurring more slowly in the South, the introduction of industry is nonetheless remaking the economic life of the section. If we consider England about to step into her new rôle and the South on the threshold of hers, similarities and differences in situation present themselves. It is true that England before becoming the workshop of the world was, substantially, an agricultural country. The South was more exclusively so. England, by handicrafts, fabricated for her own population and had some surplus for export. She already had the capitalist method in production, and it is to be remembered that the distinction between the factor and factory systems is more important socially than economically—the essential characteristic was concentration of ownership of tools and materials. Application of power to machinery followed the commercial extensions of the first part of the eighteenth century.

The South a century later had lost the thrifty domestic industry that marked colonial and Revolutionary years, and possessed, with rare exceptions, only such dwarf mills as had struggled through the blight of plantation slavery. So far from having manufactures for export, she relied upon the North for even the appurtenances of agriculture; in place of a growing commerce stimulating industry, dependence for finished goods throttled any strivings toward manufacture. The South's capital was in agriculture; statesmen and others distrusted industrial employment of funds, for such was strange, and tended to lead away from slavery; there was conspicuous absence of the corporate form of business enterprise. England through a logical, if astonishing, development, utilized her past; the South, in a no less brilliant *coup d'état*, repudiated her past.

In neither instance was the new departure into industry fortuitous; in the background of England and of the South alike were still-born inventions and trials. The stocking-frame of 1589 " remained much as it left the hands of Lee—an interesting example of an admirable mechanical invention in a non-mechanical age "; Savery took out his patent for an apparently feasible steam engine in 1698, and it is declared that " at the beginning of the eighteenth century every element of the modern type of steam-engine had been separately invented and practically applied "; Wyatt and Paul, with their machine for " spinning by rollers," were 30 years ahead of time, and Arkwright did little more than return to their model. Similarly, it is asserted that " as late as 1810 the manufactured products of Virginia, the Carolinas and Georgia exceeded in value those of the entire New England States "; before this date numbers of inventors in the South sought and obtained patents and public subsidies; later there were some little factories that need not have contented themselves with remaining adjuncts of the countryside had they not been premature, and the stirring exhortations of William Gregg with the accompaniment of singing spindles in his great Graniteville mill fell on deaf ears.

In England and in the South, when the time was ripe, the novel adventure had strength to sweep aside obstacles. Restrictive mercantilism was attenuated and disappeared there before the challenging cry of *laissez faire;* here evaporated capital and the effects of a ravaging war and political disruption, though joined by inertia and warnings of timidity, could not block achievement.

The fundamental distinction between the two revolutions is that in England the change came unannounced, while in the South it was heralded; in England the operative causes were narrowly economic, while in the South they were moral as well. Of course the South could have formed no social determination to manufacture but for England's previous history. England had been startled by what matured; the South saw ardent hopes justified. In Britain the individual and guarded adventures of ingenious workmen and middle-class merchant-manufacturers expanded into the Manchester School, which forced the country by a demonstration rather than converting it by an argument. In the Southern States, conspicuous members of the community, at the urging of the whole people, launched upon an undertaking in the success of which all were interested. In the one case the happening came first, the adjustment afterwards; in the other there was first the forecast and then the event.

That this is true was clearly shown in the respective attitudes of public bodies. The Industrial Revolution caught Parliament without a plan. British empiricism was never more heavily relied upon. This is not surprising, for there had come a new thing under the sun. In the Southern States, legislatures, press and pulpit were agog with a purpose to carry forward what had been devised. The South, made introspective by Reconstruction, mentally rehearsed her past and understood that slavery and agriculture had led to sectional estrangement, untenable dogma and miserable war; if the South was to be salvaged there must be a yielding of political pride and an honest effort to bring industry to the aid of farming in order to restore economic balance at home and also unity in the nation. Hit by a condition, England staggered, not quite knowing whether to forbid the use of labor-saving machinery and to abrogate fixation of wages by justices; the South, conducted by a theory, was eager to forswear planter particularism and, through exemption of factories from taxation and encouragement of immigration, to speed the arrival of the new day. In England the popular reaction formed slowly; in the South it sprung fullbodied from the wave, " bright and complete." In England, protests against a rising individualism were colored by Elizabethan thought for the workman and mercantilist conception of total national interest. In the South, any voices of the past spoke in behalf of economic individualism and a frayed political fancy against a movement into which the common people entered gladly. England gave over mercantilist control for *laissez faire;* the South swapped social irresponsibility for a public design. The two industrial revolutions illustrate strikingly a remark of Cunningham: "All economic problems have two aspects, the material resources which constitute the conveniences and comforts of life on the one side, and the aims and purposes which determine human beings in the use they make of these resources on the other. There is a material side, and there is a mental and moral side. . . ."

England's industrial remaking was coeval with three important wars which, through direct government demand for goods and general military exigency, stimulated the process. The South, on the other hand, started her industrial career in the midst of war's aftermaths, and encountered, and was further embarrassed by, the crises and depressions in 1873, 1884, 1893 and 1907. England's trade could thrive despite Napoleon's decrees, and her commerce with lost colonies was quickly restored after the American Revolution. Similarly, interchange between South and North was exceedingly active during the period of Southern industrial beginnings.

As has been noted, in England the impulse in textiles quickly spread and embraced iron, transportation, mining and other industries. The revolution " was one great cycle of interacting and reacting forces, no one of which could have come to perfection without the aid of the rest." The South did not experience this waiting of the steam engine upon coal and of coal-getting upon steam power, of machinery upon iron and of iron working upon production of machine tools. For the South the mechanical means were in readiness; with country roads as poor as any in England, it is true, she did not have to struggle through a canal era to the development of railways, but had the latter relatively far along at the outset. Nevertheless, Southern progress was confined to fewer phases of industrial growth, mainly attributable perhaps to the following five causes: the lack of a previous development of varied manual production and a comprehensive industrial tradition; lack of capital at home and a lingering estrangement from and distrust of the North, whence alone help could be sought; absence of established commercial connections abroad and of home demand for by-products; the presence of the raw material of cotton manufacture, which shut off the view from other undertakings; and lastly, the very fact that one industry's emergence was not dependent upon another, but specialization was feasible at once.

The Southern movement, in the sense that it answered an ambition to make up a home-grown raw material, was toward self-sufficiency, and concern was with the effect upon the section itself; English manufactures proposed to forward an economic imperialism, and drastic results to the native population did not claim early attention. The presence of the cotton in the South as contrasted with the necessity of importing it into England, thus had a bearing upon the aims of the Southern enterprise, helped determine the policies of development, and bestowed an advantage that will some day be ruling. England, particularly when mills grew up nearer the chief source of raw material, saw the importance of adding the maximum value possible through process of manufacture; Southern factories, fabricating at first only a small proportion of the crop, never wanting for supply, able to get the staple at low and unstandardized prices, and lacking technical experience, trained operatives and capital, often did more than double the value of cotton. As the number of mills was augmented, competition became keener and outside markets were opened up, more skill was mixed with the raw material. The Southern Industrial Revolution has thus pushed the North and England into finer manufactures.

The English industry was liable to irregularity in supply of fibre, as in the cotton famine of Civil War years; and even in wool, where a home product was principally used, there were fluctuations due to changes in breeds of sheep and government opposition to enclosures. Inconveniences in manufacture in the South, on the contrary, such as sudden drops in price of goods, have been due to an accumulation and plethora of raw material. The aim of the factory is still to catch up with the farm.

Changes in industrial sites were different in England and the South. In the former, manufactures shifted from the low country to the West Riding when water power was applied to the new inventions; then with the use of steam from 1785 forward there was a readjustment with respect to coal-producing areas, in which Eastern and Southern counties still had to see their arts decay. But there was no distinct water-power stage in the Industrial Revolution in the South. The great majority of mills in operation prior to 1880 were located on streams; with this date factories became a public object, and towns which had no water-power facilities wanted cotton manufactures. After a brief but spirited debate over the relative advantage of water and steam, the latter motive force was introduced widespread—not only were mills erected in the middle districts and on the seaboard, but a port like Charleston was the readier to make the attempt with steam because of advantageous freight rates on water carriage of coal. English pioneers, when the steam engine had been improved, moved their factories from isolated stream beds where labor had been difficult to get to populous towns where hands were in supply. It was easier to bring power to people than people to power. In the South it was the towns which called for mills, not mills which sought the towns. It is fairly clear that labor was rarely a consideration in the location of manufactures in the opening years of the period; it was more largely a question of where the desire for industry existed. This is just another illustration of the fact that whereas English enterprise was individualistic, that of the South was characteristically communal. English cotton manufactures, not using a domestic product, were further localized with respect to convenience in shipment, as in Manchester for its nearness to Liverpool. If proximity to raw material had any influence as between districts within the South itself, this tended toward a diffusion of mills from their first sites in the Piedmont region.

In England and the South alike, the Industrial Revolution sharpened the distinction between town and country. In the South, besides the number of places which grew up about isolated factories, many cities, smaller and larger, were stirred by manufactures from lethargy into activity. Clinton, South Carolina, and Salisbury, North Carolina, are examples. They had been merely functions of rural life; when they determined upon establishment of mills they became complementary to it.

The growth of factories in England meant a hardship to the rural population. That portion which, robbed of by-employments in cottage handicrafts, moved to the mills, was swallowed into a fearful industrialism, leaving relative independence in the open country for numbing slavery in humid spinning rooms and dense, dark closes. Those who struggled on in agriculture found themselves in the midst of agrarian changes which reduced them as surely. The progress of enclosures with attending loss of rights on commons, capitalist farming with scientific methods and increase of farm acreages, joined with the ruin of cottage employments to evict the villager or depress him from the position of tenant to that of laborer. The case was different in the South. Here there had been no domestic industry to be destroyed. Agriculture was overstocked. The price of cotton was desperately low. The Poor Whites mutely begged for an opportunity to support themselves. In many instances a prime motive to the erection of factories was the affording of employment to these people. Generally those who went to the mills were better fed, housed and clothed than ever in their lives before. Those remaining in agriculture were relieved of killing competition, found the price of cotton improving by agency of the demand of the manufactories, had a chance of rising for the first time from the status of laborer or tenant to that of small owner, and were given in the mill villages a demand for their truck and perishable farm produce.

The Industrial Revolution in England divorced industry from agriculture, but that of the South was marked by a conjunctive relationship between the two pursuits. This was because the new industrial population had been drawn from farming, almost the only manufacture was of cotton, and the section raised its own raw material. There had been a forward and backward flow between farm and factory. In the intervals between profit in agriculture through high price of cotton and profit in manufacture from the same cause, operatives accustomed to raising the staple have left the spindle for the plow, relieving impending unemployment and steadying price levels. In some instances, as at Kannapolis, North Carolina, there has even developed a regular seasonal flux. This ready cordiality between industry and agriculture had many conscious manifestations. So far from distrusting manufactures, important planters led movements to set up factories in their fields, some mill companies raised their own cotton and processed it without baling, while others purchased large tracts of land with a view to such possibility. Everywhere the operatives were encouraged to cultivate vegetable gardens and were given pasturage rights. Not a few mill workers have saved enough money to buy farms and go back to them permanently.

The English Industrial Revolution, as typified in the Manchester School, smashed the tariff theory and practice. So intimately was industry associated with agriculture in the South that the section has remained substantially, despite enormous manufacturing interests, the proponent of free trade. Almost two decades of fervid growth of the new industrialism elapsed before significant voices for protection were heard.

Both revolutions were accompanied by increases in population. The first half of the eighteenth century in England saw an advance of 20 per cent, the second half, of 50 per cent; the first 30 years of the next century added more than the whole of the preceding hundred years, and during the nineteenth century population increased four times. The northward shift to industrial districts meant that by 1800 the population was one-third urban, where it had been only one-fifth a century earlier, and the process gathered momentum. Similarly, from 1870 to 1880 the population of the seven Southern States affected by the "Cotton Mill Campaign" increased in a trifle higher percentage than that of the country generally, and in successive decades to 1910 the increase was 15.5, 17.3 (in the height of the industrial awakening), and 14.2. Contrasting 1880 with 1910, the rural population decreased from 91.4 to 84.1 per cent of the total, while the urban increased from 8.6 to 15.9 per cent of the total. In the entire United States the urban population increased hardly more than 50 per cent. Taking the percentage of Southern population in industrial and in agricultural pursuits in the census years from 1880 to 1910, we find the figures running, for industry, 10.8, 9.3, 10.8, 13.5. The average for 1880 is higher than is really indicative, because Virginia at this time had from two to four times as many workers in manufactures, proportionately, as others of the States included. The percentage in agriculture changed from 71.4 to 64.7 to 62.4 to 63.2. In England factory industry removed a positive check on population—with sheep walks banishing cottages, it had been hard to find houseroom for children, and marriages were deferred. But in the cities children could be put to work in the mills; large families were an advantage. Likewise in the South, factories placed a premium upon children, giving them work earlier than they could have been profitably employed on the farms. In England the most disadvantaged element in the population was subsidized through operation of the poor law. The rate per capita of total inhabitants mounted from 3s. 7d. in 1760 to 13s. 3d. in 1818, shopkeepers and small independent farmers feeling the heaviest imposition of a burden which, since it supplemented wages, benefited great agriculturists and manufacturers and taught to the working classes sloth and lack of self-respect. The Southern white laboring people required deliberate social measures in their behalf also, but here the better method was chosen of fostering an industry which paid its own way; if the rise of the cotton mills was partly in response to philanthropic motive, still the operatives played their rôle in its success and at the same time helped themselves out of a slough of despond. Stock subscriptions to factories which contributed to the welfare of the general community were preferable to poor rates which relieved employing entrepreneurs of their social responsibility.

As against the increase in material wealth and ability to meet Napoleon which was brought by England's Industrial Revolution, there was on the other hand " a loss of stability of every kind; England as a nation forfeited her self-sufficiency and became dependent upon an imported food supply; and a large proportion of the population, who had been fairly secure in the prospect of shelter and employment and subsistence for their lives, were reduced to a condition of the greatest uncertainty as to their lot from year to year or from week to week.'' The reverse was true in the South—the section gained in economic balance through introduction of manufactures; instead of relying so largely upon outside sources for hay, grain and meat, the incentive to produce these at home through diversified agriculture took its rise with the industrial impetus; rather than being plunged into insecurity by the advent of manufactures, the Poor Whites were rescued from their precarious situation. Penniless families trooped from the land to the mills with all their worldly goods in one wagon, " full of children and nothing else.''

English artizans saw machines shutting them out of work, so they tried to smash them. The work people of the South knew that machines were their salvation, and so clustered eagerly about the factories. In England the new methods made it possible to substitute unskilled for skilled labor; children took the places of adults. In the South there had been almost no skilled craftsmen; now there was employment for all, children with their elders. In England the men suffered most from the use of boys, girls and women. In the South with the utilization of children the proportion of women in the mills diminished, and that of men increased.

Arnold Toynbee pointed out that the end of the eighteenth century saw an agrarian revolution in England paralleling the industrial. The Speenhamland principle in the poor law, war demands, and the corn laws encouraged scientific farming as against the open-field system. If the rural population was hurt, farming method gained enormously. Societies forwarded research (in 1793 the Board of Agriculture was founded with Arthur Young as secretary), some famous sheep-shearings became meetings of important agriculturists, breeds of cattle were improved, the steam plow introduced. The number of private bills for enclosures, measuring the progress of capitalist cultivation, more than doubled in a generation. Impulse toward agricultural advance did not come so close upon the heels of industrial awakening in the South as in England. The section had purposely turned its attention from farming when it stretched every nerve for a commencement in manufacturing. Edward Atkinson, of Boston, jealous for New England's cotton manufacturing supremacy, in vain recommended to the South sheep-breeding and the planting of mulberry trees to raise silk worms. The *News and Courier,* of Charleston, with some success urged upon South Carolina a departure into cotton milling and tobacco culture almost in the same breath, it is true, but this was an exception. The movement for better farming, when it emerged, did not work through large planters who practiced the extensive method with negro laborers and share-croppers, but singled out rather the small proprietors and upper grade of tenants, belonging to classes which had been promptly pressed downward in England. Dr. Knapp and the farm-demonstration movement preached the same exhortations to the common grower which had been embraced by the great landowners in England a century earlier.

When the industrial storm broke over England, the moneyed men were principally merchants and landlords rather than manufacturers, and the latter were only slowly accorded the social status long claimed by the former. In the South also the men of means were chiefly in trade and agriculture, but, whereas in England many from the middle class became captains of industry, here the characteristic leadership proceeded from the aristocracy. England already possessed manufactures in variety from which skilled and daring workers might spring into prominence; the South had little else beside rudimentary and scattered cotton factories. Entrepreneurs had to start *de novo*. In the first years men of the type of George A. Gray, at Gastonia, North Carolina, who had been schooled in an ante-bellum mill and became a fomentor of industry, were rare. The reform act of 1832 was the outgrowth of the pulsing industrial centers, a victory for the middle classes, and meant the passing of power from the hands of landowners to manufacturers and merchants for a third of a century to come. This had taken two generations from the establishment of factories. It is interesting to ask how far the South, now removed a like distance from its industrial commencement, has gotten toward a similar transferral. Legislatures are still typically representative of agricultural interests, and business as opposed to political traditions has not importantly impressed Southern congressmen. The new man of affairs, developed in the second generation of industrialism, has been too busy to offer himself on the hustings; but that his turn of mind is making itself felt is seen in such evidences as the growth of Republicanism. More and more, too, this productive group is exercising, through economic position, pervasive social influence. D. A. Tompkins did more for the South than all the acclaimed office-holders with whatever spectacular power over the people. The English reform act of 1869 brought workers into a position of potential power. Is the day of the common man arriving in the South? Surely no more here than there will the vote alone turn the trick; concern for public education and for rural betterment would be well supplemented, in industrial districts, by trade unionism.

There was some early outcry in England against the circumstances of child labor, such as Dr. Percival's report to the Manchester magistrates in 1784, but this instance is typical in being chiefly a medical protest and local in application. The public conscience was longer in becoming aroused, obstacles being the custom, and even praise of, interminable hours for infant workers, the tradition of apprenticeship, the selfishness of employers, and a grasping trade policy. The reasons for first apathy in the South were the bitter need of the people, and the newness of industry in all its concomitant problems. Factory masters, so far from being greedy at the opening of the period, in the main were generous. They were the saviors of the country. Later, many of the same hindrances to progress which operated in England showed themselves in the Southern States. A report of a parliamentary committee on child labor in the North of England in 1816 and a record of hearings before a congressional committee on child labor in Southern cotton mills in 1916 read like one and the same document, except that operatives testified in the earlier instance and were persuaded by their employers not to appear in the later.

The first concern in England was not over long hours, but as to conditions under which children lived at the hands of the manufacturers. Thus Peel's statute of 1802, if it was the first of the Factory Acts, was in spirit an offshoot from the poor law; it applied only to parish apprentices and stipulated for whitewashing of inside walls of mills, separation of the sexes in dormitories and religious instruction of the children; 12 hours of work were permitted. The

South possessed no background of public relief—part of the working population had been enslaved, and so made no appeal to social responsibility, and another part (the Poor Whites) had been shunned. When the Southern industrial revolution came, there was no apprenticeship; entire families came to the mills intact, so that managements stood *in loco parentis* to father and mother as well as to children; there were few evils of urban crowding; farms were close enough to supply food products and to afford, in desperate case, an economic alternative for operatives; the tradition of living conditions in slave quarters had been, on the whole, good, and the entrepreneurs carried their old sense of human obligation over from their plantation system into the new industrial relationship, and were mostly eager to know their employees individually and to guard their moral character. In England a pure capitalist greed had exploited the children.

Cunningham thinks the human miseries of the English industrial revolution came not so much from introduction of machinery as from the evils of unrestrained competition following the former regulatory theory. Negatively, the South was better off in this regard; there was nothing to suffer from a breaking down, for so far from a conscience in industry, there had not even been industry.

There is no reason to believe that women were jeopardized and degraded in the South as in England earlier. Only such a community as Charleston could have fancied such a contingency as an objection to female employment in the mills. In the South the Poor Whites have not lacked in religious zeal and moral stamina.

In comparing the two developments, one recalls that English workers possessed unionism and labor consciousness prior to the industrial revolution; these were virtually absent in the South before the rise of cotton mills and have been woefully tardy in emerging since. The South had had little industrial capitalism and, before the Civil War, what with slavery, the custom of share-cropping, and plantation commissaries, not much of the wage system.

In Britain an ineffective act of 1800 gave masters and men the right to go before arbitrators to adjust wage differences. No wage disputes arose in the South in the first years, partly because of the novelty of industrial employment, partly from the sense of the communities that enterprisers were social servants in a crisis, partly since considerable payment was in kind—free houses and wood, garden plots, pastures and schooling.

The weavers of Bolton early complained that their wages had long been so low as 5s. the week against 20s. to 30s. generally in other trades, " and that the extravagant prices of provisions of all kinds render it impossible for the Petitioners to procure food for themselves and families. . . ." On the other hand, in the South, there were hardly any other industries beside cotton manufacturing with which to compare wages, and indeed wages varied strikingly from mill to mill within the same neighborhoods. Moreover, food was cheap even in the cities. In the English Industrial Revolution, the textile workers were so stunned by sudden eventualities that they could do nothing more than impracticably plead for enforcement of an Elizabethan statute in their protection. While operatives were becoming disillusioned of an old faith and were mustering strength and courage for labor organization, humanitarians fought their battles in denouncing exploiters and appealing for new legislation. In the South workers, so recently and partially divorced from the soil, have stood longer by while reformers speak for them. In opposing the Factory Acts, English industrial leaders for the most part openly advanced their standard of the *laissez faire* doctrine. Southern mill men have not generally been so honest: the selfish motive has been cloaked by professed care for the people and obscured by intermixture of the dogma of States' rights; Southern capitalism did not know that the world had moved on in a hundred years and would discover its dissemblance. One would like to believe that sometimes, in its adolescent quality—laboring under self-deceit and taking itself very seriously to the neglect of recognition of its essential character—Southern industrialism has not even known it was dissembling.

In England, with the progress of the Industrial Revolution, appeared not only humanitarianism, represented by Sadler, Oastler, Ashley and their friends, but, almost hand in hand with each other, unionism with such proponents as Place, and Socialism swiftly passing from the good-will of Owen to the fierce championing of Marx. This sequence has not repeated itself in the Industrial Revolution of the South. Here humanitarian concern entered with capitalist enterprise, the first mill builders responding as much to social need as to private ambition. But capitalism, despite continuance of and partly even through a very business-like welfare program, ere long lapsed into a strident individualism which has helped preclude to this day both unionism and socialism.

Reasons for this are not difficult to distinguish: workers and owners in the not too distant past had the same beginnings, and employers felt a duty to welcome the Poor Whites back into economic participation; there was little pressure and contiguity of industrial populations to induce class consciousness, and there had been no manufacturing background for the maturing of working-class psychology; there was usually a recourse to the soil; aristocratic traditions of control of government readily allowed the second generation of mill men, when occasion arose, to exercise an influence formerly belonging to landowners. Education has been lacking; labor has been the more easily controlled because of poor variety in industrial pursuits—unions would have to capture cotton mills or nothing; the poverty of the section has discouraged interference with enterprise; concentration of attention of Southern legislators and Southern members of Congress on political rather than economic issues has made for slow progress in legal enactments that would in themselves have helped give workers a better purchase on the situation and enabled them to assist themselves. Alleviating legislation has been made slow by technical constitutional difficulties not operative in England. There have been relatively few men of wealth, education and vision enough to act as reformers, such as England could offer; the clergy, of which one naturally thinks, could have benefited by the presence of more men like Edgar Gardner Murphy, not so intent upon dogma as to neglect economic morality and sense. The presence of the Negro has delayed workers' self-help in the South; not only has he usually stood ready to try the white man's job at the lowest wage, but laboring whites, because they were victims of slavery as much as the blacks, have shown more disposition to repose confidence in an employer as a kindly individual than in their own leaders as representing an interest different from that of the master. It seems highly questionable whether the company-owned mill village is any longer an agency of democracy in the South.

7. THE IMPACT OF INDUSTRY IN THE SOUTH [1]

The industrial development in the South is fairly new in physical accomplishment, and more recent in

[1] March, 1928.

national notice. But it is not distinctive. In its economic and social elements it repeats old experience. In fact, a strong proof of its lack of novelty is the fact that it is generally considered novel. The rest of the country is more mindful of precedents, but within the South itself there is a total lack of historical awareness.

To the people of the district which is undergoing the change, industry, and particularly the social implications of industry, seem a new thing under the sun. The South is a good deal in the position of the old colored man who had his savings in a bank that failed. He was staring in amazement at the court notice pasted on the closed iron door. He could not take in the words. He was struck dumb. "The bank has failed, Uncle," it was kindly explained to him. "Haven't you ever heard of a bank failing?" "I knowed," he rejoined, "dat dey sometimes couldn't pay back what folks put in 'em, but I ain't never had one to bust in my face befo'!"

This Industrial Revolution in the South involves not only an alteration in our manual occupations, but a revolution in our whole social habit and procedure. We are experiencing what Walter Bagehot phrased as "the anguish of new thoughts." Every country or region which, over a short period of time, has seen manufactures added to agriculture and trading, has gone through the same moment, briefer or longer. The seizure in the South is prolonged and complicated by circumstances peculiar to us.

In subtle ways we are suffering now the penalties of long ago. Old errors pursue us with new disabilities. The ante-bellum South was devoted to agriculture, and to an agriculture of staples. This statement bears unimportant modification. There were, in the last decades of the eighteenth century and the first half of the nineteenth, some manufactures of more respectable proportions than fireside handicraft. Iron furnaces dotted the Piedmont, and little yarn factories clustered here and there. These were generally the handmaidens of agriculture. They were subdued to the prevalent system, and never threatened it. Perhaps more might be said of the larger cotton mill of William Gregg at Graniteville, South Carolina, which got under way in the late 'forties, as also of biggish plants at Augusta and Columbus, Georgia, which owed something to Gregg's philosophy. But the war came to cut off the effect of these more considerable enterprises.

The Civil War exhausted the South, and the Reconstruction period soured it. During the years of Radical Rule, the resources for recovery, already lacking, were further depleted by the depression following 1873. But it is doubtful whether more abundant means would have been utilized because of the dominantly political temper of the times. The South, beaten and insulted, spent itself in diatribe and in desperate efforts at local cultural and indeed racial protection. Correction had followed so suddenly on the heels of defeat that there was no time for repentance. Pride, the South's best asset, which should have been sublimated into reflection and rebuilding, was stung and kept to the worse than fruitless office of retort.

In the early 'eighties, with the country's business fortunes repaired and Carpet Baggers expelled from Southern legislatures, self-analysis began in the cotton States. In the cotton field arose the cotton factory. Many motives contributed to the astonishing growth of mills—the desire for profit, the plan to salvage bedraggled towns, anxiety to furnish work to the Poor Whites. Wise heads saw now that Nullification and Secession had led to disaster, and the North began to be looked to as a helpmate in working up the everywhere present raw material.

Aroused individuals and communities in the South pledged their all to the erection of the new factories, and, at once finding this not enough, hastened to Philadelphia, New York and Boston for assistance. Cash was subscribed by Northern firms that would sell the product of Southern mills, and machinery manufacturers accepted stock in payment for large orders of equipment. The promotion, be it noted, came from the stricken South. Sometimes preachers fired communities to build cotton factories as the only means to salvation, through escape from despondency, idleness and vice. Civic zeal often compelled a leading figure to become a cotton manufacturer, though his calling might be that of doctor, lawyer, merchant, or planter. In numbers of cases ex-officers of the Confederate army stepped forward to lead their people in a new and strange crusade, arming them with spindles instead of muskets. And be it remembered too that the first capital came from the South, much of it toilsomely paid in small instalments. Thus the factories sprang from the South's own resolution, ingenuity and sacrifice.

At first the mills sought water powers, and these country locations necessitated the building of villages about them to receive the thousands of families of Poor Whites that poured in, from difficult mountain farm and sterile tenant holding, to take advantage of the chance to earn. The mills must supply every facility of life, since the workers brought with them nothing but their supplicating poverty. They must be housed, taught, fed, protected. When steam was used as a motive power factories could be located in towns, but here too the separate company village was the rule, for the mills brought in country people unaccustomed to contrive for themselves even had homes been available.

The enterprises were phenomenally successful. Dire predictions of the North were promptly disappointed. Production was standardized on cheap, coarse goods; the raw hands learned rapidly; glad of the chance for bread, nobody grumbled under long hours, low wages and the work of children; surplus profits went back into the ventures, to render them larger and more autonomous.

To say that the labor supply was abundant does not express the case. Workers were not being drawn from other factory employments, from home industries, or from the many occupations which we think of as belonging to towns and cities. They came from destitution, from hopelessness, from abandonment in the country. It is doubtful whether Anglo-Saxon people at any time since the Norman conquest had a lower standard of life than these. Nearly all were ignorant not only of letters, but of the elements of progressive, self-reliant existence. Those coming from tenantry in the planting districts had never handled money, but had been subjected to a credit system which confirmed their serfdom. Indeed, if they had an overlord they were fortunate, for not a few were mere squatters, hardly, it was said, above the condition of the settled Indian. Those from the mountains were apt to come from cabins mud-floored and windowless. They had not known teachers or physicians, and their preachers, well-meaning enough, were themselves ignorant, and gave exhortations which were powerless to provide the basis for social improvement. These people did not complain; they were not resentful against their fate. Therein lay the refinement of their tragedy. Much has been said of their personal independence of will, the heritage which no amount of neglect and exclusion from opportunity could quite kill. But this individual self-respect only emphasized their collective lack of resourcefulness.

When these thousands came to the new factory villages, Banquo's ghost was appearing at the feast. The death's head of the South's old short-sightedness was brought into the light. But few had the earlier wit of William Gregg to be terrified at the spectacle. All were busy in erecting and equipping mills, throwing up operatives' cottages, forming financial contacts and opening markets. Moreover, the first sufficiency in contrast to former want was apt to give the impression that difficulties had been solved. It is only in the decades since the original boom of manufactures that we are becoming aware of the complications that are deep-seated in old wrongs visited upon the Poor Whites.

While seekers of work were many, importunate, and seemingly unending in their stream from the hitherto stagnant pools of labor, the reverse was true of capital and of managerial capacity. Of these there was not enough. The South was desperately poor, and was discredited in the eyes of the rest of the country which was looked to for assistance. Had it not been for the dearth of business which preceded 1880, and which made machinery manufacturers and commission merchants welcome a new source of custom, however unrecommended, the industry perhaps could not have gotten a start in the cotton States. Home experience in the operation of manufactures was declaratively lacking. The South's occupations had grouped about the furnishing of agricultural staples enjoying a semi-monopoly and reduced, in their production and marketing, to a well-understood routine. Under the old régime, drawn up in regiments, Southern men of affairs had delivered their volleys bravely enough; but the new exigency called more largely for the skill and ingenuity of the sharpshooter. The old ranks which knew the manual of the land were now deployed, and every man must shift for himself. Persons who could calculate manufacturing costs, cut corners and contrive economies did not readily discover themselves. Had it not been that the South enjoyed great advantages for the manufacture of cotton, and without the commission firms which supplied experience in marketing and furnished much operating capital, the native lacks would have been more apparent.

It is clear that the South showed, at the opening of its manufacturing career, the elements which have regularly marked the onset of industrial revolution—labor rendered weak by need and redundancy of numbers, and capital and management dominant through their scarcity. In the Industrial Revolution in the South the potentialities of this situation were intensified by three circumstances: (1) the former institution of Negro slavery, (2) the quality of the leaders, and (3) the sectional consciousness which remained from political controversy and civil war. Each of these has profoundly affected the history of our industry, and has a bearing upon the immediate question of the protection of workers, whether through labor organization or State or national legislation.

It was slavery which dispossessed the Poor Whites, pushing them beyond the pale of profitable employment, and excluding them from social sympathy. They had no part in the scheme of things which slavery set up, except, indeed, to be a nuisance to the large planters, or a downright danger to the orderliness and subserviency of the Negroes. Under a slavery system, moreover, labor of the hands was not honorable, and attached its mean character to all who performed it. These things, which robbed the Poor Whites of assertiveness and dignity when later they came into the factory villages, were complemented by the fact that the new industrial workers did not look upon their employers with the eye of man to master. By a strange trick the Poor Whites, in the Civil War, had fought and bled for the perpetuation of a system which had been their undoing. Even in ante-bellum days " the forgotten man " was remembered at election time, and, fired by the issue of race—the effects of which he bitterly knew, but the responsibility for which he failed to ponder—he was flattered into crying up the white aristocracy and all its interests. War, in which blood of the lower class flowed with that of the upper, brought him closer to the realization of racial identity, and self-sacrifice clinched the oath of brotherhood. If anything else were needed to establish kinship, the years of Reconstruction furnished it—the sharing of a crushing defeat was followed by elevation of the quandam slave into a position of insolent power. Thus not only were the Poor Whites in the mills not mindful of their position as employes, but, as a correlative, managers and owners of factories were relieved of all antagonism and there was no element in society to represent to them their economic responsibility as employers.

The second point, the quality of the leaders, is closely connected with the first of the fact of slavery. The pioneers in the industry were generally gentlemen. Not operatives or mechanics as in England, they did not see themselves as seizing a mean advantage. Many had been slave owners, they took authority by habit, they were accustomed to be looked up to, and they were moved by the spirit of *noblesse oblige.* The duty that they had acknowledged to their house servants and field hands in the quarters to treat them with consideration, to be responsible for the supply of their wants and answerable for all their actions, was now transferred, with the fervor of a new dedication, to the inhabitants of their mill villages. The manorial lord of the early middle ages, as owner, had been also judge, teacher, monitor, all but priest, and certainly champion. The same was true of the old Southern planter, so that he, and those who shared his tradition, carried their accustomed methods over into the new calling. The factories were nursing mothers to the operatives, furnishing quite as much directly in goods and services as they bestowed in wages. Perhaps it may be said that had the owners given less, the workers might have received more. Doles from a guarded but accumulating store were dispensed with a kindness that banished protest, and filled with gratitude. It never occurred to anyone to draw the issue of economic justice. For so long the workers had had no bread that half a loaf seemed a huge meal. So far from striving for the whole loaf, there is question whether, at first, such could have been produced. With perfect naturalness the Poor Whites regarded any man who built a factory and welcomed them into his village as a messiah, and they were content if they could but touch the hem of his garment. The wage system was new to employers who had always issued rations and firewood to blacks and whites alike, and the further implications of manufacturing industry were wholly unguessed. It should not be forgotten that the mill owner stood to his workers not only in the capacity of factory boss, but of landlord as well, and thus too was the familiar relationship continued. Paternalism was the order of the day.

Coming to the third special influence upon the social aspects of the Industrial Revolution in the South, it must be realized that sectional consciousness, besides inciting to *esprit de corps,* has set up a " defense mechanism " against criticism from without, and delayed self-analysis from within. The South had been beaten flat to the ground, and seemingly was forbidden to get up; when she struggled to her knees, she was warned that she would be unable to stand erect; when she drew herself up and began to walk about, she was watchful for new threats or taunts. When the mills came to be well established, if some of their practices regarding wages, hours and strongarm methods of excluding unionism were murmured against at home, the manufacturers were excused on the ground that no embarrassment must be put in the way of material progress for the poor South. There was an appeal to sectional patriotism, not always vocal, but none the less pervasive. Just as England had protected her rising manufactures against those of other countries by a tariff, so the South regarded the North with jealousy and suspicion, and sought to defend her industry by preserving a differential advantage. A sort of Southern mercantilism held sway. Smouldering embers were fanned into flame by Southern efforts to curb the evil of child labor. The protestants, however apparent the purity of their motives, were traitors to the South and, it was urged, to the children themselves. Home champions of the children were classed with outside investigators as agents of the rival manufacturers at the North, and their findings were branded as inspired lies. When national child labor legislation was introduced, this same argument of a persecuted section was strongly brought forward by Southerners.

Besides these accompaniments of our Industrial Revolution in the South, there have been other special circumstances more or less peculiar to the section. In England, Germany and New England, industrial development took place in several, even many, fields more or less simultaneously—iron and steel, mining, ship building, and land transport as well as textiles. But in this instance few alternate employments were opened. It was harder to realize that the region had entered upon an industrial career because of this confinement of manufacture to one raw material. The proof of a general aptitude for machine methods was lacking. If workers became dissatisfied with conditions imposed in the cotton mills, there were only sterile acres to go back to. Also, there were so many Poor Whites yet unrescued from their rural state, in comparison with whom the mill worker was well off, that arguments for improving factory wages and hours met with small enthusiasm, even could anything have been accomplished, in a realistic economic view, in face of the abundant labor surplus.

Further, all the workers are of one blood with each other and with their employers, and this racial identity has obscured economic cleavage. The thought has been held to by employers and employees alike that this is a White man's industry; that this opportunity of work is to be reserved against the Negroes has further emphasized unity of interest. Demagogues, entering the mill villages at election time, have found a condition exactly to their liking—thousands on thousands of ignorant whites conveniently collected and readily aroused by their suspicion of the Negro to vote for representatives no wiser, but more cunning than themselves. They have never been stirred against the status of their own industrial lives, but only against the bogey of Negro equality. Practically all of the Southern mill workers are Protestants belonging to evangelical denominations in a section where religion, or at least church-going, has been an inveterate habit; the labor organizer from the North has been distrusted and disliked because he himself is, or certainly represents, Catholics and foreigners.

I have tried to this point to sketch the forces, universal or particular, which have made the South slow to recognize what has been taking place. Some of these influences were stronger at the opening of the manufacturing era, but others have retained their potency pretty much undiminished over the whole period. I do not excuse our backwardness in bettering the essential conditions of factory employment; I simply wish to set forth facts without a knowledge of which our economic posture in the South is incomprehensible.

Our technical progress has outstripped our social progress. The cotton manufacture in the South has shot ahead of that in the North partly because management has been alert to introduce the newest machinery and the latest methods of generating and applying power. But the advance has also been enabled by the fact that while tribute was willingly rendered to patentees and hydraulic engineers, the workers have been paid little and have labored long. It must be remembered, however, that industrial revolutions have regularly carried two transformations, one in methods of production, and the other in methods of life of the working population.

Just as we have had in the South fundamental causes characteristic of the development of industry everywhere, and superficial influences peculiar to this section, so improvement in working standards must proceed in accordance with further progress in both of these sets of forces. We may consider the more transitory and particularly Southern factors first.

The effects of slavery are being dissipated. The Negro's nominal freedom is taking on the elements of genuine emancipation. He is becoming land owner in the country and home owner in the cities. The war demand and restriction upon immigration have set him further ahead in a decade than did years of toilsome welfare work in his behalf. At least a million Negroes have migrated to industrial centers Northward, and probably a larger number have moved from the land to urban communities within the South itself. The Negro, far more literate than before and more effective as a worker, is entering new occupations. This movement, taken over a period, is bound to improve farm methods, lessen competition in the country, and increase the profitableness of raising Southern staples, all of which redound to the advantage of the mass of whites. Everything which helps the condition of the Negro at the bottom helps the Poor White next to the bottom.

Secondly, the character of Southern industrial leaders has undergone change. The second and third generations, the men active on the scene to-day, are not eleemosynary in their nature. Rather they are entrepreneurs, trained in the school of calculation, and accepting the conditions of sharp competition in world markets. This does not represent a social loss, but a gain. Since the employer is now appearing in his true economic guise, claims of worker and community upon him stand out much more distinctly than once. It is now patent that much which the pioneers spoke in sincerity on the subject of operatives' welfare, has become mere cant in the mouths of employers who claim to protect their people against themselves, or against the State.

In the third place, sectional consciousness in the South is fading out. The "Rebel Yell," still occasionally raised by Daughters of the Confederacy at their conventions, evokes in us now a tenderness for individuals who suffered in a past day, but stirs no empty pride in the grand gesture of secession. The South furnishes the continent's latest land boom, develops giant power to rival Niagara, finds its industrial stocks bought and sold on the New York exchange with those of Pittsburgh and Detroit. In the cold months the Manhattan man leaves his desk for Pinehurst as familiarly as he goes to his club in Gramercy Park. More importantly, however, the South is becoming economically a part of the nation by reason of the movement to it of industrial plants from North and West. This amounts, in cotton manufactures certainly, to a veritable migration, and asks us to look at what is happening in the underlying currents of the Southern economic eddy.

The large conditioning facts have always been, of course, on the one hand the availability of capital and enterprise, and the degree of confidence with which these could be employed, and, on the other hand, the supply of labor. The new mills that are coming South, not only in textiles but in other departments, are tending to balance the equation by furnishing more work and correspondingly taking up the labor slack. The Southern differential advantage, reaching in cotton manufactures about 15 per cent as compared with the North, and consisting mainly, but not wholly, in lower labor costs, is destined to be eaten away little by little through the action of competition within the South itself. Practically it may be said that the only advances in pay which Southern operatives have enjoyed have come from increased demand for their services, which had its effect willy-nilly; unionism, the deliberate effort of the workers, owed its measure of success to this stimulus, and subsided when demand fell away. Unless something unforeseen occurs, and anyway in the course of years, we are bound to have—through increased investment by Southern industrialists, re-location of Northern plants, and the opening of new manufactures—a sustained lift of the operative out of low wages, long hours, and the refusal of autonomy which shows itself in annihilation of his attempts at organization, and the maintenance of the company-owned town.

There can be no doubt that in the current phase the Southern factory operative, certainly in our typical industry, is exploited. He is fit for a wider diversity of employments, he merits greater leisure and self-direction, requires to be included in social counsels, and will repay a high standard of life. I believe that, however behindhand, we are now at the threshold of the second stage of our Industrial Revolution, which shall realize these objects and bring us abreast of the times. I am certain of the satisfactory outcome. Industrialism has supplied the living spark of progress in the South. We must be careful that while we feed and encourage it, we also control it, keeping the flame to a grateful glow, not letting it leap up into a consuming fire.

8. Why Cheap Labor Down South?[1]

At this writing there are probably more workers on strike in the textile South (some ten thousand) than ever before in the fifty years of the history of the industry. These strikes are in the new rayon mills

[1] October, 1929.

of German corporations at Elizabethton, Tennessee, and in cotton factories in the two Carolinas.

The next largest number out at one time was probably in 1921, in the after-war deflation period, when members of the United Textile Workers were fighting against wage reductions with backs to the wall. At Charlotte, Concord, and Kannapolis, North Carolina, and at Rock Hill, South Carolina, and elsewhere, long-drawn contests ended in complete failure for the workers.

The country is taking unusual interest in the present strikes, whether conducted by the conservative United Textile Workers (affiliated with the American Federation of Labor) as in Tennessee, by the National Textile Workers' Union, as in North Carolina, or "leaderless," as in South Carolina. The reason for this interest is that these strikes have an important bearing upon the future history of the textile industry in America. There has been some organization of labor in the Southern mills from time to time beginning with 1898, with resulting strikes, both long and bitter; but never before has so much national concern been aroused.

The strikes now in progress come at a time when the cotton, rayon, knitting and, to a less extent, the finishing industries are in migration from the North to the South, impelled particularly by the desire to avail themselves of low labor costs prevailing below the Potomac. Much as this drift in one of the country's major industries implies, the situation is rendered more critical by the generally uncertain way in which cotton manufacturing finds itself by reason of the competition of artificial silk, the lessened demand for women's cotton dress goods (fifty years ago a woman wore nine pounds of cotton and now her clothing, mostly not cotton, weighs nine ounces), and the growing ability of the Far East to supply its own needs.

If the saving in cost of production of cotton goods in the South as compared with the North, amounting to 10 to 16 per cent, is going to be diminished, it means that decay of the old textile seats in New England and the Middle States will to that extent be arrested, and the spectacular movement of mills Southward, which has gone on for upwards of a decade, will be checked.

Interest centers less in whether the Southern strikers gain their demands, than in the indirect consequences of the present outburst—whether unionism gets a foothold, whether public sentiment is aroused to effect improvement in low standards of labor.

Conjectures in answer to these important questions can be intelligent only as they consider first the query, Why has Southern cotton mill labor been conspicuously passive heretofore, in the face of low wages and long hours?

Three points of departure present themselves: (1) The character of the workers; (2) policies of the employers; (3) opinion of the public.

1. The operatives, some 280,000 of them, or 60 per cent of all the cotton mill workers in the country, are almost entirely the Southern Poor Whites. Before the Civil War, slavery pushed them out of the picture. They became tenant farmers, or "sharecroppers" in the coastal plain and plateau, or moved gradually back to the hills where they eked out a primitive existence. They were mostly illiterate. Except for a few who were engaged as overseers, those in the plantation districts were victims of a credit system of the landlords which left them little if any real money at the end of the year. Those in the mountains had nothing to sell, or small means of getting out their products if they did; they managed to live with hunting, and by scant crops grown on steep slopes. All the things which have since been said about the sloth and ignorance of the Negro were said in full measure of these Poor Whites. There were few industrial enterprises in the South then, and such as there were often used Negro workers.

When, fifteen years after the Civil War, cotton factories began to be built in the South, the Poor Whites became the operatives. The mill builders had two motives in using this labor supply—it would be profitable because plentiful and cheap, and it would be an act of charity and patriotism to give them work in their needy state. If one is inclined to doubt the second motive, he must remember that the South had just come through the Reconstruction period, when all Southern whites were drawn closely together in opposition to the Carpet Baggers and Negroes, and furthermore, a large number of persons in the local communities where mills were projected, occupying positions of importance, acknowledged an appeal to their sense of responsibility. Often, also, merchants believed that creation of a payroll was their only salvation.

These two " drives "—profit and philanthropy—have continued side by side in the history of the Southern cotton manufacturer's dealings with his workers. As time has gone on, the desire for profit has outstripped that of service for its own sake, so much so that the latter is now only a gesture accompanying the former.

The workers came as a body from the country in the beginning; as the industry has expanded new recruits have constantly been transferred from the farms, and even those families which have been for several generations in the mills have relatives back on the land with whom they keep in touch. The Southern factory " hand " has therefore had a rural mind. Industry has remained a new experience. It has been a rescue. The mills have meant release from an agricultural serfdom, and they have brought relatively certain cash wages. These two prime benefits have acted to postpone criticism of the employer on the part of the worker. The operatives have thought of themselves, with the old pride that goes with poverty on the farms, as individuals, not as members of a group or class. This was the only expression of self-respect open to them.

Many of the first mills being located on isolated water powers, managements immediately built villages for the accommodation of the tenants and mountaineers who were being drawn in as workers. The Graniteville Factory in South Carolina, before the Civil War, had offered an example of a model village after which others patterned. When mills began to use steam power, and moved to the neighborhood of towns and little cities, they continued to build their own communities of workers' cottages, partly because there were no other housing facilities, and partly to be able to control their labor. These were company-owned towns, and as years passed they became more and more elaborate, and contained besides homes, stores, schools and churches, welfare buildings, swimming pools, barns and pastures for milk cows, movies, restaurants, day nurseries, and whole social service departments.

The paternalism of the company town—systematized, all-inclusive, and at the same time intimate—has done more than any other one thing to make the workers uncomplaining and dependent. They have not owned their homes. The employer meant to the workers much besides a provider of wages; he was their religious, social, and domestic mentor as well. He charged himself with preserving health and morals in the community. Consequently the workers could not protest against low wages or long hours or the prevalence of child labor without jeopardizing their contentment in every other direction. The church and the school, not to speak of the welfare departments, have been sponsored and contributed to by the employers, and have been engines of his will and servers of his convenience. These villages not being incorporated places, inhabitants do not vote for local officers. There are no police, but rather deputy sheriffs appointed by the county but paid by the company.

The operatives in company towns have been stall fed. They have received a considerable part of their compensation in kind—gardens, medical attention, free pasturage, wood and coal at cost, and, above all, exceedingly low rents (about a dollar per room per month). They have not known what it is to live on a cash wage as such. Their wages have been so low that all available members of a family have had to work in the mill, and the companies refuse to let houses except to families which can furnish two, three or sometimes even four workers to the factory. Hence it has been hard for one or two members of a family to break away to another employment.

Living under patronage, the mill population has come to rely heavily upon the company and its agencies for supervision and relief. I do not mean that a large measure of tutelage over a long period of years has not been necessary and highly beneficial. Probably nothing less could have brought the Poor Whites back to life. But the company-owned mill village has some time since become a means of repression of the worker, consciously maintained by the employer because profitable in dollars and cents. Some managements recently coming to the South have preferred to locate in or near a town, where a special village would not be required, or have at least used the regular schools and churches of the community. Others have experimented with selling homes to operatives.

Being in separate communities has given the workers the feeling that they are different from other people. In some cases even where the mill is located in a city it has its own village, a sort of island in the general population, with its own public institutions. The butcher, the baker, and the candlestick maker look upon the " cotton mill people " as undesirable, and these factory workers have been given an " inferiority complex," which is generally dulling in effect, but sometimes, as in election campaigns conducted by demagogues who raise the issue of the Negro, gives vent to irrational assertiveness. Physical separation has made this population ingrowing. In a political and social sense it is like the results of repeated intermarriage among relatives. The people do not come in contact with common currents; they are shut off, for example, from such groups of organized workers as the South possesses, say, in the building trades.

Low wages and long hours have not allowed them the means or energy necessary for turning their attention to plans of collective self-help. In 1927 (the latest year for which there are complete figures) the average Southern cotton mill worker received a wage of $637.17, or $12.24 per week. Earnings in the North were in 1926 about 55 per cent higher than those in the South. In 1926 the average full-time hours in the South were 55.58 per week, and in the North, 51.24. The legal limit in North Carolina and Georgia is 60 hours, in South Carolina 55; Alabama has no legal limit. On the other hand, Massachusetts, the most important New England State, has a limit of 48 hours. The 11-hour day and 12-hour night are common in the South. These conditions present an anachronism the endurance of which by circumscribed workers is less remarkable than the complacency with which they have been viewed by the general public. The proportion of women and children in the Southern industry has made organized protest difficult. For example, in 1919, 36 per cent of the workers were women and 4.9 per cent were boys and girls under 16.

A considerable block of the cotton mill workers have not entered protest against their conditions because they cherish the idea of going back to the land, perhaps saving enough from their wages to buy farms. They have thus looked upon their stay in industry as temporary; in most instances their hope has flitted before them, but nevertheless the pursuit has persuaded them to endure hardships rather than jeopardize their aim. Some workers, also, have been sending money back to needy relatives in the country, and these also are reluctant to endanger their earnings.

Collective sentiment and labor organization have encountered obstacles in the scattered location of mills. The industry in the Southern States is not nearly so concentrated as in England, New England, or Pennsylvania. It reaches from Virginia to Texas, and, while plants are thickest in the Piedmont region, they are also distributed over the coastal plain and reach constantly farther and farther up into the mountains. The Piedmont Organizing Council, an attempt this last winter to educate the workers toward unionism, has had to confine itself to one district, and still has had to meet each month at a different point. A proportion of the operatives, variously estimated at from 10 to 30 per cent, are "floaters," and drift from mill to mill and village to village. This might be thought to produce a desirable effect in unifying sentiment over the whole area, but it does not, for these families are in search of a slight advantage, or move from mere restlessness.

Textile unions in the North, to which Southern workers have had to look for incentive and support in organization, have been weak and at cross purposes. Probably never have more than 15 per cent of the operatives in the industry the country over been unionized; at present the unions may contain 4 or 5 per cent of the workers. The unions have fought each other on the issue of craft as against industrial form of organization; there are some unions confined to one district, while others attempt national scope. The largest organization, the United Textile Workers, upon which the South has relied chiefly, is opposed at intervals in its conservative policy by sudden and short-lived activity of radical leaders from outside. With the drift of the industry from the North, the stable union has found itself low in funds and morale at the very time when energetic efforts are needed in the South.

The Southern industry has not yet reached its limit in labor resources of the rural Poor Whites. Between 1925 and 1927, 34,416 additional operatives were reported. Almost none of these came from outside the South, and most were taken from farming. A decade ago, when the industry had been suddenly stimulated by war demand, it was believed the supply of those who could be pulled from the plough or coaxed down out of the mountains was running short, but since then three influences have made it easier for mills to get help: the industry has been depressed for the last six years, producing under-employment; the boll weevil has driven many off the land; and there has been a general movement from country to town, greatly increasing the South's proportion of urban population. The present strikes come at a moment when there are more operatives walking the streets than for a year or so previous. There has never in the history of the industry been a protracted period when workers could not be replaced fairly readily with people anxious to get the jobs.

The work in Southern mills has been relatively unskilled and quickly learned. This, of course, means it has been hard for the hands to protect their jobs. The work, however, in recent years has been becoming more skilled and varied; particularly it has been speeded up, so that now observers declare that certain Southern operatives are in every way equal in training and efficiency to those in New England. On the other hand, with the present tendency of cotton manufactures back to coarser products, experience will probably count for less than was promised.

2. One is bound to say that the tradition of Southern chivalry is at a discount when it touches the relations of cotton mill managements with their workers. The operatives have been given an overdose of sugar in the way of village paternalism, but have regularly and universally been denied the bread and meat of reasonable wages and hours. The true attitude of the employer, not to be excused by his protest that he knows best what is good for " his people," has come out in instances of labor organization and strikes. Boasted friendliness of mills to men has proved to be a fairweather policy, completely dropped in a squall. The devices which employers have brought into play everywhere have quickly appeared in the South—the use of troops and hastily enlisted deputy sheriffs; expulsion of

organizers from company-owned towns for trespass—in the present strikes even the kidnapping of labor leaders; eviction of operatives from company houses; breaking up of union meetings; prompt use of strike-breakers (in one case, at least, Negroes); the attempt to forestall strikes and enlist public sympathy by ostensible lockouts; discrediting of leaders by arousal of racial, sectional, and religious animosity, and the spreading of ill report about the morals and designs of organizers; starvation of employees into submission. The strikes now in progress in North Carolina bid fair to add to the mill men's record another instance of victory through mere depletion of the workers' slender resources.

The trade paper editor ordinarily taken as spokesman for the Southern employers said in the early stages of the present strikes: "There have been numerous unions organized and strikes engineered in Southern cotton mills during the past 30 years, but the . . . operatives know that not one strike has ever been successful and that in almost every case, the . . . fees and dues collected . . . has (*sic*) gone into the pockets of the agitators and has disappeared with them. It is also true that most of the professional organizers have been men of such low character as to disgust the decent people in mill villages. . . . One of them who got away with considerable funds, left two illegitimate children in mill villages in one town.'' Similarly the cry of Communism has been raised by the employers—even against the American Federation of Labor—and this bugaboo still frightens a South in the early flush of capitalism.

The employers have kept the idea before the South that any checking of their program means curtailment of prosperity, and opportunity for work is so new that the public listens with the same respect shown the threats of the mill men in England a century and more ago. Managements have encouraged the maxim that the cotton manufacture in the South is a white man's industry; the implied danger of Negro invasion is supposed to render the operatives glad to hold what they have, rather than reach out for more. Employers have had a whip in the fact that they preside over virtually the only industry. There are no other jobs to go to, either locally or in other accessible places.

3. The cotton mill workers have had little assistance from public opinion. Thinking people conceived the South's problem as relief from poverty. The welfare work in the villages seemed an important step in this direction. Further, the South has always been less aware of the need for justice between classes than of the appropriateness of kindliness shown by a superior to an inferior. Graceful patronage has been all that public opinion demanded. And industry is still new in this section. The people do not know its necessary outworkings; the disturbances in industry elsewhere have come to the South as dim and unreal report. The cotton manu-

facture here, enjoying low costs of production through expensive human subsidy, has been generally prosperous, and so the ordinary fatalities of industry, for example in severe unemployment, which bring on questioning elsewhere, have not come home. The churches have either had nothing to say on the subjects of low wages and long hours in the mills, or have distracted attention from economic wrong by stressing the calamities of individual sinfulness. One denomination has employed a minister in the heart of the textile district to bolster the welfare programs of cotton mills and deprecate collective bargaining by the operatives.

Colleges and universities privately supported have been too anxious to get funds to run the risk of alienating possible givers by forthright analysis of industrial conditions. State schools have been fearful of curtailed legislative appropriations. Professors in large numbers know the facts and would like to draw obvious conclusions, but they feel that their jobs are at stake. In a few instances, however, there has been hopeful improvement in frankness recently. Newspapers have been largely absorbed in politics rather than in discussions of labor matters, but during the present strikes more courageous statements have come from the press than from any other quarter.

How long will it take for all of these disabilities of workers to disappear to the point where we shall

have recognition in the South that we are no longer
only an agricultural society, that we have opened
our arms to capitalism, and must develop the usual
methods of rendering it wholesome for all concerned? An additional vexation in the answer is the
likelihood that, when improvement for white workers comes, ten million Negroes may be turned to as
a new labor resource—a group large enough and
needy enough to invite repetition of the whole painful process of industrial betterment.

II. RECENT LABOR UNREST

9. A New Voice in the South[1]

The American Federation of Labor, in its organizing campaign in the textile South, has two tasks before it. Which is more difficult is hard to say. One is to remove the inferiority complex of the employes, the other to remove the superiority complex of the employers.

Each has a definite background. The operatives are only beginning to emerge into self-determination, and to claim a voice in public counsels. They are the Southern Poor Whites, descendants of the stepchildren of slavery. They have no purchase on economic life, but have been like golf balls knocked about a putting green until they fell into a hole. All of them formerly and a portion of them until recently, have been attached to the land, but either they owned not a foot of it, or what they possessed was worthless. If they were tenants on a plantation they swapped promise of labor for credit at commissary or country store, and their crop netted them little cash in hand at the year's end.

If they owned their little places, these were apt to be mortgaged to the hilt, and they derived little besides a meaningless pride of possession. A mule

[1] April, 1930.

and a bull-tongue plow were their instruments of production, and the more cotton they grew the worse was their plight. Those in the mountains enjoyed an empty liberty, which consisted more in idleness than in material sufficiency.

Fifty years ago the first of them came to the new cotton mills in thousands—unlettered, beggars for bread. The eagerness and rapidity with which they learned a new routine of industry shows how bankrupt was their past enterprise. By necessity they placed themselves in the hands of the factory owner, and he accepted responsibility for maintaining and reshaping their lives—in work, in play, in thought if there was such, in morals. Asking everything, contributing only compliance with orders, they demanded nothing. Any stirrings of revolt met their defeat, not in the employer's opposition, but through the workers' own gratitude for his service to them in their extremity. Thus the employes.

The employers in the cotton-mill South come by their superiority complex quite as naturally. Historically, they are aristocrats. The first mill builders, who rescued the post-Civil War South from the poverty of a disrupted agricultural system, were men of family or position, often of both. The fact that they alone had plans and the contrivance to carry them out, would in itself have marked them as figures of distinction. They supplied the essential boon for a broken people—the opportunity to work. The reward they reaped was adoration. If anything were needed to clinch their position, it was furnished in the response of the common people to their complete paternalism. I use the word in its pure sense. It was fatherhood. The Poor Whites under slavery had been excluded, while slaves were cherished. Now the disinherited were read into the will. They had been starved, now they were subsidized. They had been unnecessary, now they were all-important. The bond of sympathy between whites of both classes was cemented against the common enemy, the Negro. The factory owner, by tradition, through economic mastery, and as racial champion, went unquestioned.

To the esteem in which the manufacturer was held was added his own consciousness that he was the means of survival, and beyond that the engine of progress. Not that he was thirsty for admiration. He was too busy about the works which deserved it. He grew into humility which is the high counterpart of lordship.

Gradually the adventure proved itself. The mills were successful, and as the technique—financial, mechanical and commercial—became familiar, plants increased in numbers. Apprehension gave way to security. Ambitions that had been sustained by hope were now established in good fortune.

By insensible degrees the employers began to presume upon their position. Welfare work which had been ingenuous was undertaken with the design of attracting operatives and keeping them contented at low wages with long hours. Owners boasted of their social services to their workers. When labor unionism first showed its head a generation ago there was no difficulty in putting it down; few of the public thought the operatives could have a legitimate protest against employers so benevolently inclined. The same favorable conception of the proprietors' character, aided by pressure which they brought to bear, served to quiet local stirrings against the abuses of child labor, but were not sufficient to avoid federal inquiry and condemnation of the evil.

The first real thrust at the employers' immunity from attack came during the World War. For some years previously labor had become scarcer, and now wages rose, because the cotton farmer was getting his tardy innings on the land, men were drawn off to cantonments and munition plants, and the mills enjoyed spectacular prosperity. Thus the workers as a group became convinced of their importance to the industry, and two score thousand in the Carolinas joined the union. The organized workers, however, lost their strikes against post-Armistice wage cuts, and the employers sat almost as firmly in the saddle as of yore. Almost, but not quite, for there was still the vivid recollection of unionism in the minds of the people.

Then a lull, until the Southward drift of Eastern cotton factories aroused attention, gathered force, and then became one of the great movements in the history of the industry. These Northern mills came seeking cheap labor primarily, and their arrival brought new problems—increased demand for workers, further dilution of the welfare motive, weakening of the old sectional defenses for low labor standards. Simultaneous depression in the industry was responsible for the introduction of an alien efficiency device, the multiple loom or " stretch-out " system, by which the workers were required to tend more machinery without always being compensated in number of helpers and increase in wage.

So came the series of strikes beginning last spring, which took out 17,000 operatives and found highwater marks in Elizabethton, Marion and Gastonia. Two of these major strikes were organized only after they had begun, and all of them caught the responsible labor leaders perforce without plans or fighting resources. In the autumn the United Textile Workers appealed to the American Federation of Labor for aid, and in January of this year at Charlotte, North Carolina, President William Green launched the South's first widespread organizing campaign.

The issue is now fairly drawn between an outworn tradition and the new need for workers' representation. This is neatly apparent in the current passage of arms at Danville, Virginia. The Riverside and Dan River Cotton Mills, some dozen plants (one of them a few years ago claimed to be the biggest cotton factory under one roof in the world) have

467,000 spindles, 13,000 looms, 5,000 workers, and assets in excess of $25,000,000. The president and treasurer is H. R. Fitzgerald, who is to be accounted a comparatively enlightened Southern cotton manufacturer. He has had extensive welfare work, but in addition, a decade or so ago, he introduced John Leitch's company union plan known as "industrial democracy." Mr. Fitzgerald doubtless believed that his position was not only irreproachable, but that he was a benefactor of his workers and, in a perfectly proper way, an example to other employers in the South.

The present writer had some correspondence with him when the company union was inaugurated, pointing out the imperfect protection which it gave to the workers, and suggesting that it would not answer in a crisis. But he was unconvinced.

The company paid 6 per cent on its preferred stock and 10 per cent on its common; in 1929 in order to do this three-fourths of the payment to common stockholders had to come from surplus. Wages were reduced 10 per cent. Soon the workers showed a dissatisfaction which would not limit itself in its expression to the company plan of labor representation. Operatives held organization meetings.

Mr. Fitzgerald posted a notice addressed "To All of Our People." It began:

We are informed that paid organizers have appeared in our midst, and that, as usual, they are appealing to such prejudices as they can arouse. . . . Our system of employee representation contains every element of collective bargaining that has any real merit. . . . We do not desire the employees of the company to be misled by these outsiders for the simple reason that they cause discord, and their whole method of operation depends upon agitation and strife. . . . What can such a movement do for you that you do not already have except to take your money in dues to pay a lot of foreign agitators. . . .?

Mr. Fitzgerald declared that the organizers want the money of his people not only for union purposes, but " incidentally, to fill their own depleted coffers."

All of this is a regular enough remonstrance of a late representative of the Old South. The surprise is in the answer it promptly elicited from a meeting of the workers. The men have been doing more thinking than the management. They rejoined:

First of all we want you to know that the American Federation of Labor and the officials of that organization came to Danville at our request for a union. The representatives who came here are not foreign agitators but American citizens delegated by President Green . . . to assist us. When you say their whole method of operation depends upon agitation and strife we would call to your attention that the officials of the labor movement have advised the workers in your mills to keep calm, that the American Federation of Labor is not here for strife or strike, but to organize the workers and do business in an orderly manner with justice to employer and employee.

And they went on to recite the failure of the company union to protect them, closing on the note, " We are sending this letter to you in good faith, and ask you to accept our offer of friendship in all sincerity."

This reply of the Danville operatives marks an epoch in the history of Southern labor. Here is a calm putting aside of the old sanctions—without hysteria, with the minimum of bitterness, with eyes to the future. Capitalist industry everywhere has experienced three phases—first, revolutionary increase in production; secondly, elevation of *laissez-faire,* with the accent on individual bargaining; thirdly, humanitarian revolt against exploitation, formation of labor unions being the most important item in this program. This letter proves that at least some in the South have reached this third phase, and that industrial relations in that section can never be quite the same again.

The cotton manufacturers of the South must manage to exchange a patronal relationship to their employes for a contractual one. This lesson has always been learned at the cost of lives, money, social cleavage. The South must remember this history, and in the years that lie next ahead seek to avoid it. Several circumstances lend hope; the employers, in their claim to be considered moralists, are assailed by their own misgivings, and the public is less credulous of their professions than it once was. The counterpart of the Southern workers' long patience in the past is undoubtedly conservatism and reason for the future. And not least in importance is the fact that the present organizing campaign, particularly in the face of depression in the industry, has adopted and proclaimed the engineering approach to the whole vexing problem.

10. FROWNING AT THE SOUTH [1]

The North, the world indeed, is frowning at the cotton mill South. The American Federation of Labor at its Toronto convention has just resolved to raise funds for a concerted drive to organize the Southern operatives. The Cotton Textile Institute, formed to help lift the American industry out of its depression, has developed a rift between its members above and below the Potomac. A New England manufacturer in the annual meeting has sought to oppose the Institute to night work for women and minors in the South. Five years ago Massachusetts cotton mill men, citing the Southern differential advantage in lower wages and longer working time, appealed to their own legislature for an extension of the 48-hour week. Since then, be it noticed, the design has changed. In the first instance the New England manufacturers wanted to lower their standards toward those of the South. This took no account of overproduction that might result. In the present case a surplus of products is the immediate stimulus, and it is proposed to appeal to the Southern legislatures to curb the working time of Southern factories.

[1] November, 1929.

The International Labor Office is preparing to make an inquiry into the depression in the world's cotton and woolen industries, in which conditions in the South must play a large part.

The current strikes in Southern cotton mills have called forth a yelp of protest from workers and liberals in the Northern states. Strike relief funds have been collecting, large meetings have been held and more are planned to acquaint the North with the low labor standards prevailing in the South. The rest of the country, while less active in indignation, is learning the facts as to the South as never before. High-powered writers whose eloquence claims a national following have rushed to the South and are now busy syndicating their articles. The British newspapers have been avid for information about the progress of labor's fight against the 55- and 60-hour week and the 14-dollar wage in the mills below the Potomac. A score of Irish and Scottish textile manufacturers, just arrived in this country to study our industry, will find the difference between labor costs in North and South the problem most pressed upon them.

All of this is significant. It means that for the first time the South is being measured against national and world industrial standards. The depressed state of the cotton industry, due mostly to overproduction and diversion of taste to other textiles, has brought this outcry against the South.

The ship's company would appease the storm by searching out the Southern Jonah, and casting him overboard.

Leaving aside the rest of the world, what can the North do to improve labor standards in the cotton mills of the South?

First of all, in any activity designed to raise the manufacturing costs of their competitors, the Northern mill men must meet hostility and suspicion. This is rooted in the past. The secession complex has not been dissipated; at every sharp brush between sections it shows itself again. Industrial development in the South, while it has brought the section nearer to Northern interests and ways of thought, has furnished occasion for the opening of old wounds. A quarter of a century ago, when child labor in the Southern mills was upon the carpet of national investigation and Northern humanitarian protest, Southern manufacturers were quick to claim that investigating agents were sent down by jealous Northern competitors. Labor unions attempting to organize Southern operatives were credited with being financed from Northern mill coffers. Southern enterprisers still get a hearing when they exclaim to their public, " We lifted you out of the poverty that followed upon the Civil War—it is your patriotic duty as Southerners to protect us in the social subsidy which enables us to keep going!" Like the British cotton men of a century ago when beset by parliamentary correction, they threaten to tumble their factories down if hindered.

Special dislike is reserved for the Northern textile unions. It is pointed out that they are headed by foreigners, Reds, Catholics; that they stir up strikes in the first place only to take membership money out of the South. Most of such argument is disingenuous on the part of those who put it forth, but the general public is ready to believe a great deal of it.

A second disability of the North is the delicate position of its own textile manufacturing interest toward the South. Many Northern mill men can scarcely decide whether to stick it out in the North and exert themselves to remove low labor costs in the South, or to desert a sinking ship by moving their machinery to the low-paid, long-worked crackers and sandhillers. While there is a chance of their deciding upon the latter course, they do not want improvement in the South, but the reverse. Furthermore, other Northern firms are already astride the fence, with plants in both sections. These, many of them the largest companies, are to be regarded as backing the Southern horse; their equipment in the North will be moved South with little additional provocation, and they will be lost to the Northern opposition.

The position of organized labor is not equivocal like that of the manufacturers. The unions have every motive to raise labor standards in the South. By doing so they protect their Northern membership against the low bid of the Southerners, which has been taking bread from their mouths, and they also acquire strength in the region to which the industry is demonstrably drifting. Their embarrassing weakness flows from two quarters. First, the unionists are divided in their own ranks between the National Textile Workers (Communist and, for all the fact that it is largely on paper, bold in its methods) and the United Textile Workers (affiliated with the American Federation of Labor and more moderate in demands and practice). There are other union groups, their bonds being by craft or regional propinquity. Secondly, at the very time when the United Textile Workers, best equipped in experience and membership to organize the South, needs money and morale for its task, its Northern strongholds are crumbling as mills move South and set their operatives adrift. Furthermore, the distance to the South and the differences in race and language between Northern and Southern workers, not to speak of the union tradition of the former, make it impossible to shift these dispossessed ones in pursuit of their machines. Added to all is the fact that less than 3 per cent of the cotton mill workers of the country are organized.

This is not the end of the union's disabilities. Hostility to organized labor in the South, which does not attach only to managements and owners, but pervades a large section of the cotton mill operatives themselves, would indicate the wisdom of using Southern men as organizers. But in textiles these may be said not to exist. Union men from the building trades or officials from the State and city federations have been drawn in to assist with strikes, but these lack specific knowledge of the industry and are often not of the locality involved. In the recent strikes reliance has been placed upon young organizers from the North, who, despite courage, ingenuity and perseverance in the face of staggering difficulties, have been handicapped by unfamiliarity with the habits of their immediate adherents and, more important, have not been able to make an effective appeal to Southern public opinion as a whole.

Everyone recognizes, except perhaps the Southern strikers immediately involved, that the recent and current conflicts are really battles between the Northern and Southern branches of the industry. This has increased the amount of false report on both sides. Northern organizers, returned from the South to seek support, tell traveler's tales of the Poor Whites—men with one suit of overalls, ancient women and half-grown boys and girls toiling in the lint-laden, humid atmosphere of the factories, impoverished villagers nailing together pine boxes to contain their dead. Their audiences, heretofore looking upon the Southern Poor Whites only as picturesque natives to be glimpsed about Pinehurst or Aiken, are now moved to pity or consternation. The Southern mill owner, set forth as an obstinate and callous ogre, awakens indignant reproaches. They all seem as far away as the Arabs of Palestine, and therefore the imagination has full play.

On the other hand, the Southern mill man is apt to paint the Northern strike leader and all his sponsors as scheming, conscienceless liars, animated by the spirit of the fiendish Trotzky, if not financed from Moscow. Both sides, talking of strangers, stretch their fancies.

Feature writers, some of them with names to flag any reader's interest, transcend this back-and-forth imprecation of combatants with a practised and one-sided eloquence. They are apt to remain just long enough at the Southern scene of action to learn little but see much, and what they see, ground through the journalistic mill, comes out as moving copy. These high-minded reproaches are convincing of national scandal. These accounts are the siege guns of the labor war; they score few direct hits, but their boom is alarming and they carry many leagues.

One who is acquainted with the history that has brought the South to its present pass, and who knows the limitations of strikers and mill managements, feels like protesting the superficiality and artfully concealed sensationalism of these reports. They are stagey things, mere cardboard sets, but probably they are inescapable, and in the wide polemic of industrial betterment, they have a certain admitted place. Social reform has always required the cartoon as well as the table of statistics.

At a meeting of New York liberals a fortnight ago to discuss the industrial conflict in the South, competent observers and old hands at the labor game urged the audience to get " a little crazy " to see the workers win. There are many temptations, mediate and immediate, to this counsel, but I wonder how much an outraged Northern social conscience, with the best intent in the world, can do to bring a solution in the South. In the face of working conditions that cry out for remedy, with all too few friends on the side of enlightenment, one hesitates to recall the ancient warnings about the slow patience of social change.

And yet here, as elsewhere, they hold. It does not alter the case that long hours, low wages and absence of union recognition in the textile South represent an anachronism. None of the factors in the present situation has come into being suddenly. The Southward migration of Northern mills, which has precipitated the conflict, was long in preparing; it began two decades ago and for years has been foretellable in its acceleration. The bad hours and low wages, and the employers' " welfare offensive " too, have their roots in the competition of the Poor Whites with Negro slaves a hundred years ago. The individual manufacturer, whose plant may be struck, is part of an industry unusually competitive sectionally, nationally and in world markets. He, no less than his operatives, is caught in a vise which will be relaxed only by practised untwisting of the screw. Pressure must be applied with knowledge.

To be specific: here is a Southern cotton mill which has been struck all summer. There have been incidents enough—in poverty, suffering, violence—to excite sympathy and financial support for the workers. The management becomes more and more exasperated, and redoubles efforts to install strikebreakers. As a consequence, evictions from the company houses to make room for newcomers loom as a new source of friction. An agreement is reached and broken, each side charging the other with the first show of bad faith. The mill begins to fill and the situation of the strikers becomes more acute. Each of the contending parties believes bad things of the other, and reports worse. Perhaps outsiders who attempt to mediate eventually become partizans on one side or the other, and add to the confusion.

Labor standards in the factory are undeniably low. The mind of one a little detached runs ahead, however, for an answer to the question, How much, leaving aside the personal equation as expressed in aggressiveness or stubbornness, can the striking workers really expect to get? Let us suppose this mill is making shirtings of a given grade, and that its product amounts to 2 per cent of that of the whole country; that is, of every 1000 yards of these shirtings manufactured, this mill turns out 20. Suppose further that 90 per cent of the competitors of this mill are working on the same hours and the same wage-scale with it. If this struck mill has a safe surplus laid by, it may accede to the strikers' demands, planning to meet the increased cost out of surplus, and meaning before this fund is expended to shift the old man of the sea from its back, or to speed up the workers or make adjustments in equipment or product which will enable it to carry the burden. But in any event, the prospect before the mill, if it is to give in, is not exhilarating. It is not disposed to accept a handicap in the cost of production, and trust to the future. In the realm of practical bargaining the union faces limitations which may not be dispelled by emotional appeal.

The best course for the union would be to bring pressure to bear on all the manufacturers of shirting of this grade at the same time. This is a counsel of perfection which the restricted funds and scanty membership of the organization have heretofore, at least, rendered impossible of realization.

Southern manufacturers as a whole, as compared with those in the North, enjoy a differential advantage of 14 to 16 per cent in cost of production. If this differential could be wiped out by union action, voluntary response of manufacturers, legislative limitation on the working time, or by all of these methods, bringing the South to a parity with the North, it might have the good result of raising labor standards, lessening the amount of goods turned out, and improving the quality of product. This attempt is well worth making, but the whole situation is charged with inertia, and always in the shadows the cheaply operated oriental mills loom like goblins before the Southern manufacturer of coarse goods; for they are injuring his markets more and more.

It seems fatuous to turn from the crack of a deputy sheriff's pistol in a mountain mill village of North Carolina to the world textile inquiry being made at Geneva, and expect an answer. And yet help from some such source is not chimerical.

The North may get " a little crazy," but more potent for assistance, and more impressive in its righteousness, will be a spreading awareness and maturing sentiment in the Southern public itself. Here lies some immediate hope. A pervasive pressure from Southern public opinion will facilitate the large number of seemingly unconnected betterments, which, taken together, will speed solution. Indignation from without must melt into anxiety for remedy at home if the thousand troubles that stand in the way of improvement are to be got over.

Once the South comes to understand that it has manufactures as well as agriculture, a factory proletariat as well as a rural peasantry, that capitalism is crowding upon the older culture, and that this section is now incorporated into a national and world economy, the dangerous gauntlet of industrial adjustment will be run, at once with the necessary caution and courage.

11. Taking a Stand in Dixie [1]

The current strikes in the textile South have dispelled an illusion of the American industrial enterpriser. This was that the Poor Whites of the South, unlike labor elsewhere, never knew when they were put upon. They are, as has been widely advertised by Southern chambers of commerce and power companies, 100 per cent native born; they are Protestants and religious; they do have in the main a rural background; but they are not utterly passive. There are some fifteen thousand of them on strike now in Tennessee and the Carolinas, and those in South Carolina came out in a leaderless protest.

The causes of the strikes fall under two heads—the superficial and the underlying conditions. The strikes themselves are of more importance than the demands of the strikers. The workers are not asking for improvements chiefly, but for the maintenance of the established practices. Thus their thinking is negative, not positive. The strikes are an outburst of emotion, and not a result of planning.

The immediate occasion has been the multiple loom or, as called in the South, the stretch-out system. It was introduced by Northern employers who have entered the South in the last half-decade. It is a method of speeding up work by requiring weavers to operate more looms—in an extreme case 124 instead of 18 as a few years before. Everyone allows

[1] June, 1929.

that this policy was inaugurated without tact. To set a Northern efficiency man with a stop-watch to calculate the wasted time of a Southern operative without previous consultation was almost certain to lead to indignation on the part of the operative, particularly when it resulted in a conspicuous increase of his work with little increase of his wages. Employers are now paying the price of thoughtlessness in the method of instituting the scheme, and of unfairness in distribution of the benefits.

Workers in the rayon mills at Elizabethton, Tennessee, want a few dollars a week more, and those at Gastonia, North Carolina, besides abolition of the stretch-out scheme, are ostensibly asking for a minimum wage of $20.00 per week, but strikers in South Carolina make no protest against rates or hours. In view of these facts it may appear inconsistent to give superior importance to low pay and long hours, and yet these have been the occasion of restiveness and will be one of the determining considerations in the history of American textiles in the next few years.

The Southern textile industry—in cotton and rayon, in spinning, weaving, knitting and finishing—has grown astonishingly in the last few years because of both expansion from within and migration of factories from the North. The latter has been one of the most conspicuous drifts in the whole history of industry. The latest government figures (for 1927, but just released in preliminary form) show that in cotton manufactures alone the cotton-growing States had 61.9 per cent of the establishments of the country (59.2 in 1925) 60.2 per cent of the number of wage-earners (55.5 in 1925) and turned out 57.5 per cent of the products in value (54.2 per cent in 1925). The cotton-growing States have certainly half of the spindles in place in the United States (48 per cent in 1926) and well over half the active spindles (57 per cent in 1926).

The South consumes about 30 per cent of its own cotton crop, or two-thirds of the total consumption of American cotton by American mills. Between 1925 and 1927 the New England States lost 9312 cotton mill operatives, and the South gained 34,416. North Carolina, the leading Southern State, has 5000 more operatives than Massachusetts, the leading New England State, and products worth $25,000,000 more. In addition, $100,000,000 has been invested in rayon plants in the South—mostly in Virginia, Tennessee and West Virginia—within the last few years.

The progressive decay of the cotton manufacturing industry in New England and the Middle States, and the migration of mills to the South, is principally due to low wages and long hours below the Potomac. The average earnings of the Southern operative in 1927 (the latest complete figures) were $637.17 a year or $12.94 a week. Hourly rates for the four leading Southern States were, in 1926 (according to samples collected by the government) in North

Carolina $.28, South Carolina, $.25, Georgia $.25, Alabama $.24. Northern earnings in 1926 were 55 per cent higher than those in the South, despite a shorter working week. The study last quoted shows that average full-time hours in the five leading Southern States were 55.58, and in the five leading New England States were 51.24. The legal limit in North Carolina and Georgia is 60 hours per week, in South Carolina is 55 hours and Alabama has no legal limit. No Southern State forbids night work for women, and the 11-hour day and 12-hour night are common. Of 15 Georgia mills reporting in 1926, six worked 11 hours five days and five hours on Saturday, and six of 47 reporting in North Carolina did the same. Massachusetts, the New England State hardest hit by the southward migration, permits only 48 hours a week and no night work for women. Southern children 14 and over may, with exceptions in North Carolina and Alabama, work the hours of adults.

Consequently, it costs less to manufacture cotton in the South than in the North. In a typical Southern mill running 55 hours, in 1926, the cost of manufacture was 16.8 per cent less than in a Massachusetts mill running 48 hours; this is $6.73 per spindle, of which $4.53 is attributable to saving in labor. The Southern mill saved 33 per cent in taxes, the same in power, and 25 per cent in maintenance.

All of the Southern mill operatives have a rural background. They are the Poor Whites, ejected by slavery from economic participation. Those in the rayon plants of Elizabethton are working in factories for the first time; many of them still drive to and from their mountain homes daily. Those in the Carolinas have for the most part been in the mills for several generations, and a larger proportion than in Tennessee come from the lowlands. The striking workers in Tennessee have joined the United Textile Workers to the number of 3500. This union has several advantages—long, but sad, experience in the South; affiliation with the American Federation of Labor, a foothold in the North, and good discipline. Mainly for these reasons it is less bold than the National Textile Workers' Union which is guiding the strikes in North Carolina, centering in the Loray mill (owned by Northern capital). The United Textile Workers are sending Southern men as organizers among the South Carolina strikers, who previously have had no outside leadership.

Whether or not the strikers get their demands at this moment is less important than whether unionism gets a new start in the South. This is not the first attempt at organization of the Southern factory hands. At intervals from 1898 to 1921 there were organizations and strikes; in the latter year (after which almost complete subsidence of unionism followed) there were about 9000 out, almost as many as at present. The strikes which have taken place in the last six weeks have shown that the Southern worm will turn, and this has given comfort to Northern manufacturers, who begin to sing that the Southern labor honeymoon is over. If unionism can consolidate its position, the southward trek will be noticeably slackened.

The likelihood is that when the smoke clears a large local of the United Textile Workers will be found at Elizabethton, with defeats elsewhere. Nevertheless, these strikes will have been everywhere successful. Already they have rung the knell of the grosser forms of exploitation of the Southern mill operative. Publicity far greater than labor protests in the Southern States ever had before has lit up what was being done in a corner. Southerners aware of the low labor standards prevailing in the section, who have been trying for years to get the facts out, now find valuable allies.

To such students and friends of Southern industry a little epoch was marked by the report of the South Carolina legislative committee, albeit the chairman is the president of the State Federation of Labor, to the effect that the true cause of the strikes is overwork and underpay of the people. This legislature had not been distinguished for frank statement before. Now that the seesaw of competition between Northern and Southern mills has been tipped in favor of the South, and it is demonstrated that this is to be the predominant seat of the industry, obstacles to national recognition of the submerged state of the Southern operative are removed. Formerly the Southern mill man, with great local influence over press and pulpit and politics, entered no campaign for labor improvement. Protests from Eastern manufacturers were confined to attempts to lower labor standards in New England; there was no real attempt to save the situation in the North by bettering conditions in the South, partly because many enterprises had sails all set for flight to the South, and did not want to see waves kicked up in the new haven they had determined upon.

Now that the majority of the mills are in the South, and competition within the section will be ever keener, inhibitions will be removed. In the present state of cotton manufacture, what with the entrance of rayon and the enormous diminution in quantity of cotton goods worn by women, coupled with the growing ability of the far East to supply its own needs, the struggle of the individual plant for survival will be active. Northern and Southern managements within the South will not be able to work together in presenting a united front against labor and against public opinion. Employers of the two sections have been organized in separate associations, the relations between which have not always been friendly. These enmities will increase rather than diminish now that individuals of the two groups are bedfellows.

Furthermore, there is coming to be a plethora of cotton mills in the South, and the anxiety to capture new ones will turn to suspicion of adventurers from the North who come down to profit by low wages and long hours in the South. Competition for the most skilled and steady labor will be brisk, and the proportion of " floating " workers, which has been a bar to unionism, will diminish. Fewer companyowned villages will be built; these have fostered the " welfare offensive " of the employers. Workers living in the general community will not be so stallfed, and will own their houses and develop other ties to hold them in one place. Overproduction is already calling up a demand on the part of the employers for abolition of one of the abuses of the industry, night work. The Poor Whites in the mills are becoming literate; in the present strikes the United Textile Workers has been impressed with the fact that whereas 15 years ago many more than half those who joined had to make their marks, the great majority now can write. This in itself forecasts an end of economic passivity on the part of the workers.

All in all, a change is arriving in public opinion. Editors of Southern textile trade papers who have in the past been nefariously, or at best blindly, partizan, are now intimating that employers in the stretchout system have pushed their workers too hard, and are in danger of killing the goose that laid the golden egg. North Carolina has just passed an excellent workmen's compensation act. This was rendered possible partly through the activity of professors in State schools, which are deserting the classics for the study of industry and business, and are alert to local conditions. The fact that important Southern States voted Republican, North Carolina and Tennessee among them, has worked an emancipation of mind. New and varied industries are developing in the South—paper, furniture, cement, iron and steel—and these will dissipate the cotton mills' grip on labor and legislative protection.

The steel strike of 1919-1920 was lost, but public opinion won many of the workers' demands. The 12-hour day and seven-day week, formerly defended with confidence on every ground, were doomed through publicity. So from this time on in the textile South there will be more and more concessions by employers. Wider breaches will present themselves to the entrance of labor organization, and another industrial swamp will be gradually drained.

12. Haymarket and Gastonia [1]

Samuel Gompers, who was not extravagant in statement, said that the Haymarket bomb of May 4, 1886, not only killed a few policemen but destroyed the effectiveness of the American labor movement for a number of years. This riot, resulting in hanging for the "Chicago Anarchists," was a tremendous burden to a conservative, constructive leader such as Gompers, who was just then setting about the work of the peaceable American Federation of Labor.

[1] August, 1929.

Will the killing of Chief of Police Aderholt, of Gastonia, North Carolina, on June 7 and the coming trial of 16 unionists charged with the deed, have a like effect upon the labor organization in the Southern textile field? To the mind of anyone familiar with the history of labor relations in the industry and the attempts to improve the workers' standard of living this shooting must appear as the most melancholy of happenings.

To begin with, it requires a degree of industrial experience and sophistication to distinguish between the mere incidents of unionism and the exciting forces back of the movement. The South at present does not possess this economic sophistication. It knows much more about violence in general than about the true purposes of labor organization or the causes which have called it into existence. A murder trial with 16 defendants, where the victim was a chief of police, is calculated to set every literate person reading, though a large part of these Southern readers will have had no idea of the conditions at Gastonia which gave rise to the strike led by the National Textile Workers' Union.

The labor and capital conflict did not become really militant in the South until after the World War, when wage decreases set the operatives, organized in new thousands, to defending the gains they had made. Very soon mills from the hitherto dominant Northern textile centers began drifting to the South, slowly at first and then in a rush which has sapped

Massachusetts, New Hampshire and Rhode Island towns of their old prosperity, and given Philadelphia an awful apprehension. This Southward trek of the industry has lately redoubled efforts of Northern workers to organize below the Potomac, now not simply, as once, to enlarge the membership of the unions, but to save their very existence.

The Southern cotton manufacturer, and to a degree the Southern people as a whole, their governmental officials included, have about the same exaggerated fears of unionism as were entertained in England a hundred years ago. The South has reached the point in its Industrial Revolution which England had reached then. The "monstrous sentence" of the six Dorchester laborers to seven years' transportation for the mere act of combining in 1834, though it excited tremendous indignation on the part of organized workers, brought only tardy retreat from the Government, and was not sufficient to prevent a decline in labor aggressiveness. Three years later Chartism, itself childish enough, it is true, threw the ruling classes and their spokesmen into a still more childish frenzy against risings of the people.

There may be an important difference between England then and the South now. Probably conservative Britishers were genuinely alarmed over labor demonstrations—not only on account of their own interests but for the welfare of the social body as a whole. The quick appeal to the common law would indicate as much. But there is reason to believe that the shock and anger of the property-owning South is not so naïve, but is assumed as a regulation tactic. It is hard to be sure of this. The Victorian young lady may have fainted because her stays were too tight, and not for effect. Surely, the Northern manufacturers who have recently come South, as in the case of the owners of the Loray Mill at Gastonia, must have difficulty in giving their outraged virtue the appearance of spontaneity. These, in their fight against the union, are tilting with an old enemy. Only the links are new. The gallery has not seen a wicked knight unhorsed by Galahad before, and so the whole show assumes the guise of novelty. It is always unfortunate when a labor dispute ends in violence, but it is doubly lamentable that a killing should have marked this particular strike at this particular place of Gastonia. The inspiration of the National Textile Workers' Union is Communist. The demands of the union for the workers at Gastonia were not extreme. On the contrary, they represent good sense, and their forthright announcement argues the courage of the leaders. The only rashness has been in inaugurating a struggle which the organization had not the membership nor the funds to prosecute over a period of time in case the opposition of the employers did not crumple up. But the name of Communist frightens Americans anywhere, let alone in the South. The connotation is sinister. The real facts escape notice. The Communists are a small band distinguished by conviction and energy, their vices being impatience and a willingness to use fair means or foul to knock the props from under more conservative and conciliatory labor organizations. They are numerically weak, and finance their projects on a shoestring.

The fine-yarn center of Gastonia has had a spectacular rise. Blessed with a farseeing promoter, George Gray, in the 'eighties and 'nineties, who drew about him others hardly less talented, the town linked prohibition with business and determined to replace every distillery with a cotton factory. From this grew an air of righteousness, to which was added extraordinary technical proficiency. There is no other single community in the South with so many spindles in a like area. There are exceptions, of course, among the mill men of Gastonia, but generally their spirit is Bourbon beyond that of others. They are strident, and hold correction in contempt. The place is entirely industrial, having none of that culture and disinterestedness which emanates from a group of old residents, as in Greenville, Columbia or Augusta, recruited from the professional classes and retired planters. It presents but one facet to the protest of workers, namely, the fighting front of capitalism.

In the coming trial we shall be told all the actions and words of police and strikers—the force of every blow, the vehemence of every curse. And the scenes in the courtroom of Judge Barnhill will be portrayed with zest—the color of the jurist's tie, the gestures of the attorneys, whether the bailiff seizes upon the right or left arm of a prisoner. It would really be more to the point if the South and America could, out of this trial, somehow get it into the mind that the average weekly earnings of cotton-mill workers in the four leading Southern textile States were in 1927 (latest census figures) $12.83, and that the average hours of these workers are about $55\frac{1}{2}$ a week. Despite every precaution there will be tragedies so long as we have grade crossings; and while cotton-mill operatives are underpaid and overworked in the South there will be from time to time a chief of police or a striker with a bullet in him. Bad labor conditions in the mills mean a half life for thousands much more to be deplored than a quick dispatch for this contestant or that one.

13. THE COTTON MILLS AGAIN [1]

It is fairly certain that this year will see another attempt by the United Textile Workers to push unions into the Southern cotton mills. Both the American Federation of Labor and the Women's Trade Union League have shown themselves disposed to help in a campaign and various outside bodies have studied the problems likely to arise. If the union succeeds in building a number of large

[1] July, 1927.

and stable locals the results will be important for the whole cotton industry. A step will have been taken, too, toward control of the conditions under which industrialization in the region shall proceed. If the union drive fails, the South will have its cherished peace for another four or five years; but failure is not apt to have a deeper meaning.

Campaigns have been made in the South ever since the industry got under way. Southern manufacturers, and some Northern ones, content themselves with the shop-worn explanation that the organizers come down at such times as they think the Carolina villagers are prosperous enough and gullible enough to provide a fattening sum of initiation fees and dues for the New York treasury. The motive is not as simple as that. The American Federation of Labor, recognizing with the United Textile Workers that strong cotton mill locals must be the backbone of any real development of the labor movement in the region, helps largely with that fact in mind. The union itself is anxious to increase by a Southern membership its preponderance over the independent textile organizations, hastening the time when they will have to fall in with it. It exhibits also a righteous wrath about feudal villages and welfare workers and union-hating mill barons. The governing motive is probably that of relieving the pressure on Northern wages and hours.

Since 1920, the long-booed-at Southern competition has been a stone wall against progress for most of the Northern cotton workers. With mills dribbling away to the South each month, many New England employers are trying hard to "restore equality" by depressing labor standards. Where the 48-hour week or prohibition of night work are in force by legislation, manufacturers plead for repeal. Wages are nibbled at from many angles. Doubling up of machines and adoption of the multiple loom system proceed with disregard of the protests of the union. This pressure is mainly the result of the status of labor in the Southern mills: its long hours, meek flexibility and wages low to a degree not entirely accounted for by smaller cost of living or balanced in the mill books by the expensiveness of village perquisites. There are other attractions, but the Southern advantage is essentially its lower labor costs. The union does not expect that a lucky Carolina campaign will enable the operatives to gain at a jump the New England scales, but it does hope to begin in the South the process of union jogging and stiffening of standards that will lessen the gap between the two regions more rapidly than if the section were left to itself.

If this year's invasion meets the hoped-for response it will be the third or fourth time that unions have spread into the Southern mills. The Knights of Labor in the later 'eighties led a few strikes in Carolina and Georgia mill villages. Ten years afterwards, roughly from 1898 to 1902, a good many thousands of the people went into the old International Union of Textile Workers. Its 40 or more Southern locals, with a Georgia president, provided a whole string of towns with strikes. When the old union merged with the new United Textile Workers, then controlled by unambitious craft bodies, outside support was withdrawn and the Southern movement wilted in harsh defeats.

In 1914, with the United Textile Workers shaking itself free from localism, a bitter dispute in Atlanta gave national publicity to Southern conditions, setting a series of union-conducted strikes to popping through South Carolina and Georgia for the rest of the war period. With the ground thus broken, the 1919 wave of unrest swept more people into the union than it was prepared to manage. North Carolina signed up thirty-odd thousand workers and South Carolina and Tennessee at least another 5000. A widespread reduction in Southern hours coincided with this drive. Members had begun to drop out when the 1921 depression came, but Southern union enthusiasm was still strong enough to persuade the United Textile Workers to sanction, with suspended benefits, a last stand against the successive wage cuts. The three months' strike of 8000 people in the heart of the Piedmont area proved once and for all that union action on a big scale is possible in the South, though the strike itself was a dying effort. Since the collapse of that year a dozen tiny locals have been revived, with a district council of their own, but with a total membership that is almost negligible.

What the union needs is not spasmodic strike organizations, but strong, permanent locals in at least some of the strategic places. For a good many reasons the business of getting them is as hard a trade union problem in strategy, persistency, and power as the country provides to-day.

The mill workers of the South are 300,000 Rip Van Winkles. Slavery and cotton penned them in the untaught poverty of the back country for four or five generations. They know less about union meetings, negotiations with employers or strike discipline than the immigrant workers of Lowell or Lawrence. Deep prejudices—sectional jealousy, bitter Protestantism, and a stimulated Anglo-Saxonism—add difficulties for a Northern, partly Catholic and somewhat non-Nordic union. As yet the Negro is of little direct importance, though he is a rock on which a union movement might in the future easily be wrecked.

Employers have special and non-technical reasons for opposing unionization. The paternalistic attitude which produces the company town demands undisturbed loyalty for its working out. The great Southern mills, from motives more commendable than questionable, are set upon improving the condition of their operatives with as much educational and welfare work as stockholders will agree to. A vast amount of good has come from the system. Naturally, the men who are directing it see a union as a monkey-wrench in the machinery. Even were it not certain that unions would weaken or remodel the welfare movement, mill owners would combat the organization of a people whom they believe to be intellectually too immature to use power soberly.

The company-owned village gives the mill-men two lines of defence. A silent, smoothly-working pressure to keep people with suspected "industrial philosophy" out of each village or to suppress their union leanings after they are in, is maintained through the tenant relationship. A good Southern superintendent knows, or can get for the asking, intimate facts about any of his people. Once a local union has been exploded into a mill community, the employer can fall back upon his extraordinary powers as owner of the settlement. In a strike he can evict, arrest through deputies paid by himself, forbid trespass to organizers, prevent distribution of literature, close meeting halls, influence merchants to refuse credit, even array local mill-subsidized ministers against the union. He need not always overtly exercise these powers to make them effective. Wholesale eviction, for instance, is seldom carried out because it shifts sympathy to the workers. But in a pinch they are available to break anything but the most strongly entrenched organization.

General opinion in the region is strongly against any extensive unionization of the mill workers. Several circumstances set the middle class against the cotton mill unions—civic shame in the occasionally violent outbursts of discontent, business losses, the possible brake on industrial growth for a particular town which permits unions to become domiciled, sectional feeling plus a distaste for the character of some of the organizers who have blustered through the region. Many agree with the employers that the process of redemption from neglect has not yet gone far enough to make release from paternalism wise or to make unions of a sort different from the old strike gangs possible.

But the basic difficulty lies in the surplus of labor. Except in times of the greatest activity, a large reserve of hands is drifting from village to village. It is usually only a matter of days or weeks until mills can be filled with strikebreakers.

Lastly, Northern textile unionism is notoriously of the thinnest. Scarcely 40,000 of the three-quarters of a million textile workers outside the South belong to unions at all. Even this membership is split into two uncooperative camps, with a dozen small independents struggling in local areas. The United Textile Workers has never been able to afford the large sums that continuous organization in the South requires. Its campaigns have been successful only when and as long as help came from the American Federation of Labor. For such time as disunity prevails in the North it is difficult to see how the efforts in the South can be other than intermittent, unless the impossible happens and some campaign sets off a self-supporting movement among the Southern workers.

At intervals for 30 years union agents have been coming back to New England after a scouting tour in the South with reports that the region is "ripe for organization." It is easy to see some of the things that lead the union this time to believe that it can at least find a few mellow spots. The depression of 1920 came just when it looked as if success had been finally won in the South. The union expected the bad times to be only a temporary interruption to its progress. Now, with prosperity of a sort back in the Southern mills, it hopes to gather the threads dropped six years ago. Something is left of the network of partially trained leaders and the thousands of union sympathizers. Not a few villages still have charters waiting in attics until reorganization comes.

A number of skilled textile crafts, one under the jurisdiction of a powerful Northern association, have come into the region. It is possible that workers in these by-industries may assume a position of leadership like that of the mule-spinners of New England, who for many years "fought the battles of the textile workers alone." The United Textile Workers, remembering the manner in which the difficulties of 1919-21 were met, must have been helped in deciding many tactical points: what towns in the region offer it the first chance of success; whether it will gain most in a new attempt by emphasizing or smoothing over craft lines in the mills; what are its best channels for giving publicity to its program (it will miss Barrett's now defunct Charlotte Herald, which provided back-talk from the operatives to the views of the less tolerant employers); whether, if the campaign is successful, it will do best by encouraging a wildfire spread into isolated villages or by building a solid core of membership in the more completely industrialized towns. Certain elements of Southern opinion, there is reason to believe, will be more suspicious of anti-union propaganda than in the early post-war years.

And in the time since the last collapse in the South, the United Textile Workers itself shows signs of a subtle change. Less is heard about its "militancy" and more about its "readiness to cooperate with employers." The new official policy of the American Federation of Labor was leavening the textile union four or five years ago. The influence within the union of the progressive organization of full-fashioned hosiery operatives, an infusion of the new unionism from the extinct Amalgamated Textile Workers, and a closer tie with the workers' education movement have led the union to emphasize a phase of peaceful labor tactics hitherto neglected in the strain of endless conflicts. It was the exclusive attention of the union to its fighting side that so antagonized Southern employers.

The new cooperativeness is as yet by no means paramount in the organization, but if it grows it may provide in the South an escape from the old rigid alternative of abject labor dependence or recurrent labor war.

These changes since the last big effort make it possible that the United Textile Workers will have a fair field to show its best performance in the South. But a few false steps in the struggle of a developing campaign may still wreck the drive on some wholly irrelevant matter. Again, it is possible that internal quarrels or a persistent lukewarmness in the Southern workers may cause the union to retire without shooting its bolt. Such an abortive campaign was launched and withdrawn in 1923.

14. A Wave of Strikes [1]

Elizabethton, Tennessee, is quite a town these days. Not a year ago Mr. Hoover used it as a platform from which to speak to the whole South. It has two big mills that make artificial silk, built in the last two years by one of the German companies, and employing several thousand hands. Here is what it was like in 1860: it had a postmaster, an innkeeper, and two merchants. Its name was pronounced Lizzi Bethton, and the signpost on the Tennessee side of Iron Mountain read TOEBIOM—" to Eliza-Bethton, 10 miles."

[1] May, 1929.

Now it is a focal point for the labor movement in America. One of its mills brought in an efficiency engineer who was to teach the people how to dispense with extra motions in their work. Two hundred of them went out, and next day 5000 were parading. Union organizers flocked in, " like vultures at the smell of carrion," said the employers' journal. In something over a week the head of the biggest firm gave in and the operatives were to come back with an open-shop agreement (*i. e.,* with membership in their union at least not officially forbidden to the workers) and with concessions in wages.

But excitement in the town continued. Eight motors, filled with picked and pistol-bearing business men of that end of Tennessee, appeared at the door of the hotel where the organizers were, sent in a committee to assist with the packing, and convoyed their haul into North Carolina, whence return would carry death. Companies of the Tennessee Guard helped out the new militancy of Lizzibethton. Some hundreds of operatives nevertheless joined the union. Now the mills are " closed indefinitely."

Elizabethton started something. Another strike against the stop-watch broke out in Greenville, South Carolina. People who we are told are " Communists "—the term in America means anything from a diffident critic of the cautiously " constitutional " American Federation of Labor to the genuine imported Russian—entered the Piedmont country, fifty miles above Greenville, and led a series of strikes in such up-country mill towns as Gastonia, Pineville, Bessemer City, and Lexington. In Gastonia, National Guardsmen have been camped inside the mill's wire fence for weeks. Recently, in the same town, some 50 masked capables of North Carolina, not to be outdone by their public-spirited fellows of Tennessee, led a dawn attack on the Communist headquarters, but found their victims flown, and could only show their good intentions by wrecking the building. Meanwhile the operatives in some of the towns hesitate between a return to the benevolence of their employers and a step along the adventurous path of organization à la American Federation of Labor.

These are queer doings for the South. The white operatives in the mills are the descendants of the class that slavery pushed aside. They are the same group whose loss of standards is so tragic in contemporary South Africa. But 50 years ago the South set herself to redeem them, and used cotton mills as the agent. From farms and from the mountains the people pushed into the mills as fast as they were built, until by now an industry about the size of that of the Oldham district has been fostered. Now that the stoppage of immigration has cut off the stream of new arrivals that the Northern mills had accustomed themselves to living upon, the South holds the last pocket of cheap labor in the country. Money wages in the Massachusetts mills are at least 25 per cent above the cash payments in most of the South, and the cheap rental of the company-owned houses and the perquisites of village life do not make up the difference. Hours are 48 in Massachusetts, 55 or longer in the Carolinas.

Naturally the Northern operatives have done their best to push their unions into the South. Robert Howard, who left his Stockport mules to become the strongest leader American cotton workers have had, tried his hand in Georgia in 1897 and failed utterly. The American Federation of Labor followed him up, and failed. When the United Textile Workers had won a little strength in the North it looked Southward, and led strikes all through the war years in Georgia and South Carolina, but it had nothing to show for it all in 1918. In 1919 there came the boom, when over 40,000 of the Southern operatives did join, but they pulled their officers with them into a despairing strike in 1921, and then abandoned unions as things unattainable. No amount of campaigning since has stirred these Southern workers until now.

If in this wave of trouble the unions get a foothold it may mean a good many changes, immediate or remote, in the cotton industry in America and in the position of the mill people. For the industry it would almost certainly mean a considerable shortening of the hours of labor in the South and the prompt ending of night work, which some of the employers are already anxious to do away with. Wages would probably rise a little. These changes might have the promised effect of slowing the decay of the New England industry, but one is doubtful of that; the South's advantage in labor supply will compel continued rapid growth there. For the mill people the entry of the unions would be the beginning of the end of the industrial feudalism by which every visitor to the mill villages is struck.

15. Blundering Along in the South [1]

Anybody who went into the cotton mill villages of the Southern States three months ago would have been told by every employer and every petty boss he met that the people were contented, had no wish to work shorter hours, and considered their wages good. Most newspaper editors would have said pretty much the same thing.

A few men in the stronger universities understood the formless desire of the operatives for more liberty and better conditions; a handful of alert ministers knew of it, too; but the South as a whole scoffed at the idea that in the sunny villages, with their rows and lanes of neatly-painted houses, their roaring mills working through the days and nights, many people were "discontented." Was not the South startling the whole nation with the pace of

[1] May, 1929.

her industrial progress? Were not the mill operatives earning ten times more than they had ever had in cash on their miserly tenant farms? Did they not have clean houses, good schools, well-filled churches, baseball teams, recreation rooms—all the equipment of fuller lives than many of them cared to live?

Yet sharp practices and injustice and driving went on beneath the surface, and no man spoke. Employers and their friends knew that the tension of the work was being tightened, perhaps dangerously; but their rôle demanded silence, in the hope that what was being tried would be "put across." That is one of the pities of the situation in the South—that no organization has existed to see that changes follow lines which seem reasonable to the operatives, and no newspaper gathers the views of the workers, and sends them into the shallow pool that is Southern public opinion.

The driving was "stretching"—the application of the multiple-loom system. Under the direction of efficiency experts a number of mills began the elimination of waste motions on the part of the workers, coupled with an increase in the assistance given the weavers, and a lengthening of the alley tended by one operative until it included some scores of looms. Where the pay was raised it was raised only a little, and sometimes the earnings stayed the same. Some of the experts used harsh methods and bad language, and in one big mill in Elizabethton, Tennessee, a hurried walk-out of 200 mountain-bred workers resulted.

That sort of strike has happened many times before in the South. Usually it can be hushed up by a talk from the mill owner, who gathers his people about him on the ball field; or else a respected citizen and a newspaper editor will get the facts and smooth out the trouble. But this time there was electricity in the air. Across the mountains in North Carolina, a powerful little union of silk-hosiery knitters had been dogging the heels of the 20 or 30 employers who had built mills in the South to escape the union rates of Philadelphia and northward.

The knitters had breathed life into the State Federation of Labor, had conducted a series of little strikes, had paid their benefits in some cases for a year, and had sent Southern knitters up to jobs in union shops at three times the wage they received in Carolina. These men had paraded through Carolina towns in their Northern-bought cars, urging union. Virginia unions and Carolina unions met. Every month for a year or so a Piedmont Organizing Council has planned for the great campaign.

Elizabethton workers took up the flame of unionism. Two thousand odd operatives followed a day or so after the first 200 had struck. Next day more thousands had left another mill. The mills were both big artificial silk plants, built in the mountain town within the last two years. Union organizers came in, signed up a few members, and in a little more than a week got the people back, with wage increases and a promise of no discrimination.

At the same time a similar, but smaller, strike broke out in Greenville, South Carolina. Within a few days more strikes were popping in North Carolina towns, most of them quickly settled. It was certain that the South was in for some lively weeks, but the strength of the agitation was greatly increased by a sudden piece of cowardly folly by alleged business men of Elizabethton.

The town was growing and its suburbs reposed comfortably in the hands of real estate agents. If the unions got a foothold it might mean no more mills for Elizabethton. It appears that the real estate agents took arms in gallant defence of their economic expectations, commandeered a collection of local preachers, policemen, and more business men, and in a procession of eight motor cars descended on the hotel where the union's representatives were staying. The leading organizer turned from a conversation into the sights of a couple of pistols, and was forced to pack his luggage and climb into one of the cars.

A drive of some miles carried him to the Tennessee-Carolina line, the use of tar was significantly explained, and then, with a volley of pistol-shots over the organizer's head, he was sent into the next State and threatened with death if he came back. Later in the night the other organizer was kidnapped in the same way.

Union man No. 1 telephoned to Washington, to the President of the American Federation of Labor, as did union man No. 2, and before many hours all three went back into Elizabethton, appealed to the Governor of Tennessee for protection, and put the union on a sound footing. Now a guard of Tennessee mountain men, armed with long guns, goes about with organizer No. 1.

That piece of silly advertisement probably put the union into Tennessee for years to come. It may be that, after so many failures in the past, this wave will be more than a wave, and that Eastern Tennessee will date its effective unionization from Organizer Alfred Hoffman's midnight ride.

Meanwhile in Carolina a strike at Gastonia, in a cotton mill, had brought in the Communists. In all the big strikes in the Northern textile mills at Lowell, at Passaic, and at New Bedford, a few active Communist leaders have competed with the American Federation of Labor union for authority, and among the immigrants of the Northern cities the Communists have had their share of the honors. But in the South, where if at any place individualism was supposed to be pristine, Communist leadership is at least anomalous. Gastonia "business" men could not stand the strain; they wrecked the building where the strike-leaders had their headquarters, and did it while companies of the State troops were camped inside the mill yard. But the leaders were not dislodged. In Elizabethton, too, discrimination against union operatives has brought one of the mills to a standstill again.

The United Textile Workers of America, which is the recognized union backed by the American Federation of Labor, has had a long experience of Southern strikes, and knows the weakness of the position of the operatives there as well as the intensity of their resentment of anything they consider oppression. It knows, too, how easy it is for Southern excitement to give way to years of union apathy. Yet in spite of the difficulty of the Communist competition it has resolved to give every effort to making the present agitation in the South result in permanent unions. It is only a strong, democratically-conducted organization that can bring out in the Southern operatives the independence they have through poverty neglected, and give to them the practical, every-day liberty that an outsider admires in the Lancashire achievements.

16. Steps in Union Progress [1]

I have been interested for the last few years in the question of trade unionism in the South, and particularly in the textile industry. I have made some study of the long series of attempts that have been

[1] June, 1929.

made to implant a labor movement in the Southern mills, from the first enthusiastic strike of the Knights of Labor at Augusta, in 1886, to the forlorn resistance of 1921, and the feeble efforts that have been made since then. The least acquaintance is enough to produce the certainty that the present months are crucial in the history of the movement.

I should like to point out some of the wider and more distant events that one may reasonably expect to depend upon the fate of this union drive, and to urge that the mill workers do the few simple things that are necessary for those changes to become possible.

In the first place, the immediate objects of the trade union agitation can be secured.

No reason whatever exists why Southern mill operatives should not work on a 48-hour week. Night work will go with very little effort. Wages can be increased, though in what degree no man ought arbitrarily to predict. People who join trade unions should not expect all of these objects to be attained to the full in a few months. They will come more easily in quiet times than in troubled. But trade unions will bring them quicker than anything else.

Secondly, the economically wasteful squeezing of the New England textile industry can be lessened. It is nationally hurtful to bring mills to the South at a rate more rapid than is warranted by the advantages which the South possesses in climate, geographical position, or capacities of mill officials and operatives. Improved standards in Southern mills should enable the Northern industry to resume the progress which it was making before 1920 toward granting the conditions of labor which obtain in advanced European countries.

Thirdly, a powerful educational influence can be brought in by the mill workers. A by-product of trade unionism no less valuable than better hours and wages is the alertness which union members show toward conditions and events and movements in the outside world.

Men and women in the South today are carrying forward a school system which offers the best of civilization to the people. The usefulness of that system can be multiplied many times by the interest which is necessarily shown by every person concerned with the success of a modern labor movement. Mill people must have experienced in the last few months the educational stimulus that comes in the wake of their economic effort. A permanent movement would impenetrate the whole Piedmont with men and women interested in a variety of projects of social improvement. These people would be listened to or laughed at, as mill workers chose.

A weekly newspaper, devoted mainly to news of the Southern industry and its operatives, would be circulated in every union village. Such a paper in

England, the Cotton Factory Times, has been for 40-odd years the lever of progress. Contrast the value of a paper like that and the sheets about company tea-parties and family visits that Southern employers issue now.

To get the most out of such a union side-program of education it would be necessary to get, either by law or by trade union action, perfect freedom of meeting in mill villages. Nobody can point to a good reason why school buildings should not be opened in every mill town in the South to meetings of trade unions or other bodies. Schools in England are used for purposes of that sort every evening of the week. Classes for grown people carrying the spirit of Workers' Education, teaching plain economics, showing the progress of labor in the past and in other countries, and giving a place for the most thoughtful people in the mills to argue out the future of the industrial South, could be established in every up-and-coming city and town. Southern workers would find the spiritual wealth of the whole world-wide progressive movement poured, without thought of reward, at their feet.

Fourth, on trade unionism could be founded, if Southern workers saw fit, a political movement. I do not know the intricacies of the political forces in the Southern States, though I understand something of their delicacy. It is plain to everyone, however, that at least in the more industrialized States, wealth rules, though it is answerable, clumsily, to public opinion. But the public opinion that counts is that of a small proportion of the middle classes.

Progress could be speeded up a great deal by making the wishes of the educated industrial and farming people effective.

It is believed by many thoughtful people that the expression of the finest things in the American nation awaits the growth of a party that can effectively oppose domination by money. If that is true, the industrial South perhaps has it in its power to contribute heavily to the nation's finding of itself. One can catch a vision of the South becoming again a source of leadership and encouragement to the whole country.

These four results of a permanent trade union movement are things that can quite naturally happen. Roughly, they are what has been achieved in every country in which unionism is strong. To set the future of the South in this path it is only necessary that cotton mill people should do two things: (1) Join a sound trade union, and pay good stiff dues, month in and month out, from now on. (2) Give earnest care to the running of the local and general union, in particular by selecting honorable, capable people as officers.

17. American Textile Unions Past and Present [1]

The close relationship with the English unions which American textile unions have always felt has

[1] July, 1927.

had a new prominence in the recent visit of President Thomas F. McMahon, of the United Textile Workers of America, to Lancashire and Yorkshire.

To English trade unionists the comparative youth of the American unions must be an outstanding characteristic. The earliest organizations, the " associations " of mill girls in the New England towns in the 'thirties and 'forties, died when the Yankee girls gave way to Irish immigrants. Unionism was not active again until 1858, when English cotton mule-spinners in Fall River began their long struggle to spread organization through their craft and among the workers about them.

By 1886 the battle had been won for the spinners, and they had taken up their honored place as leaders of the movement in the American mills. Meanwhile, a belated counterpart of the Grand National Consolidated Trades Union, the Noble Order of the Knights of Labor, had swept thousands of textile craftsmen into loose assemblies, and when in 1885-90 the Order broke into fragments it left groups of textile workers who had had a few years as labor unionists. The hosiery workers, carpet weavers, jack spinners, and many of the craft bodies of Fall River and New Bedford trace back to the days of the Knights. In all this early period English and Irish workers had been prominent as union leaders, and some of the lodges were at first branches of Lancashire unions.

In 1890 the American Federation of Labor made an effort to unite the scattered textile unions into a single National Union of Textile Workers. Very soon a rift appeared between the strongly craft cotton locals of southern New England and the more "industrial" operatives of the Middle States. In 1895 the craft men withdrew, and began the organization of a loose federation of unions on the English model. After five years of limping, the industrial remnant, strengthened by a sudden burst of unionism among the backward workers of the South, prepared for a new amalgamation. Under the guidance of the American Federation of Labor it succeeded in bringing the English craft union men and a few small independents back into a general union organized as the United Textile Workers of America.

But the re-organization came at the cost of a disingenuous compromise. The constitution gave the power to the central officers, but the low per capita tax kept the money in local treasuries. For 15 years the new textile locals tried to win the old New England cotton workers over to centralization, and in the end adopted for themselves what they wanted and let the craft men cut adrift again. That left the field in 1915 divided between the United Textile Workers and the body which later became the American Federation of Textile Operatives; the first the recognized union affiliated with the American Federation of Labor, and the second a "dual" union, branded by the United Textile Workers as "behind the times" and "ultra-conservative," but with a sturdy tradition of collective bargaining on the English plan in fine goods cotton centers, and with a stable membership of little less than the United Textile Workers could claim.

Through the war years the bickerings of these two rival textile unions weakened the whole movement, but as war conditions ran up the membership in the industry the United Textile Workers grew to 10 or 12 times the size of the craft federation. In 1919 a third union entered the field. Neither the United Textile Workers nor the American Federation of Textile Operatives had ever reached the mass of unskilled immigrants. A new Socialist union, the Amalgamated Textile Workers, set itself to cross the language barrier and bring in the unskilled. By the middle of 1920 the three large unions had a total membership of perhaps 220,000, with the United Textile Workers leading. Outside any of these bodies there still existed ten or a dozen small craft or by-industrial unions, mostly in and around Philadelphia and New York.

As membership slumped in the years of depression the perplexing variety of textile unions cleared a little. The Amalgamated died a mayfly's death. The United Textile Workers dropped to a body of 30,000 skilled and semi-skilled operatives, mainly in cotton, hosiery and wool. The American Federation of Textile Operatives drew within its original Fall River and New Bedford shell. The various independents formed a paper alliance as the Federated Textile Unions of America, and took part in unsuccessful but still pending negotiations for fusion with the United Textile Workers. Today the field is divided between the 10,000 craft unionists of southern New England, who still refuse to be swallowed in a centralized organization; the 20 odd thousand mixed industrial members of the United Textile Workers of America, and the eight or ten thousand members of independent unions of silk workers, lace operatives, machine printers and the like.

The main difficulties in the North have been the vast numbers of immigrants, the scattered nature of the industry, the lowness of counts spun, and consequently the small number of highly skilled operatives, and the failure of leadership to arrive at a plan of organization acceptable to all the unionized workers.

The rapid growth of the cotton industry in the States of the South has brought not only a tremendous problem in extending trade unionism to the workers there, but also a serious obstacle to union progress in the North. Since 1880, the New England area has been losing mills to the South. The chief attraction there is the labor available from a curious pocket of impoverished white farmers whose forefathers were pushed by the slave system into the region about the Alleghany mountains. These operatives are working today at wages from 10 to 30 per cent below the scales in New England. Their hours are from 55 to 60 per week, while most of the Northern workers are on a 48 hours week. They have scant protection from their State legislatures. The cutting off of foreign immigration has given Northern manufacturers the alternative of paying high wages to the relatively scarce labor about them or moving South and paying low wages to the still plentiful " Anglo-Saxons " of the Carolinas and Georgia. Lately the New England manufacturers have been streaming South, and the Northern operatives are feeling the pressure of " Southern competition " in earnest whenever they apply to their frightened employers for improved standards.

In that situation the obvious remedy is to organize the South. Unless it can be done the Northern workers would appear to be in for long years of impotence. But the 200,000 Southern workers are about the most difficult people to unionize of all the workers on a difficult continent. Unions have darted through them, much as with the English agricultural laborers, but next to nothing remains of active organization. The operatives live in company houses on company land, they are isolated physically and culturally from the people about them, they are racially, sectionally, and religiously prejudiced against many of their fellow-workers in the North, and they are constantly under espionage and indirect pressure from a group of bigotedly anti-union, albeit professedly benevolent employers. It is remarkable that in 1920, 50,000 of them were members of the United Textile Workers; it shows that they have the spirit of the English operatives to whom their employers so frequently compare them in efficiency and in descent, but in the face of the odds against them they will have a hard struggle to build up unions with the stability of those of Lancashire.

Some things favor the Southern textile workers. Highly skilled and powerfully organized crafts, such as that of the full fashioned hosiery workers, are going South with the cotton mills; diversification is opening up new occupations in textile and other manfacturing employments; agriculture is improving and lessening the reserve of labor; wages are slowly rising and hours decreasing; education is letting the operatives recover the heritage that isolation lost them. When these forces have gone further the Southern mill workers should be in a fairer way than their Northern fellow workers to unroll again the story of English textile unionism.

At present the three big problems before the American textile union movement are—(1) a joining of forces among all the Northern unions on a basis of give-and-take as concerns old prejudices; (2) increasing the stable membership in all branches of the textile industry (there are not more than 40-odd thousand trade unionists among the million textile workers in the United States and Canada); and (3) the planting of permanent unions in at least a few points in the South.

18. IN THE SOUTHERN COTTON MILLS [1]

"Mr. Hoffman, we are going to strike."

"There isn't a cent of money for relief, fellows," said Alfred. "You can't strike now."

"Hell!" said the committee, "we've done struck."

Marion, North Carolina, where the union committee made this historic remark a few weeks ago, is one of the lesser "show places" among Southern cotton mill villages. Last year its owner arose in a labor meeting and challenged a critic of Southern paternalism to come to Marion and hunt for dissatisfaction.

It follows Elizabethton, Greenville, Gastonia, Ware Shoals, and a dozen other places in showing the rebelliousness of the Southern Poor White millhand. Fifty-five and 60 hours a week, long night shifts with a full staff of women, an average cash wage of 45s. a week, company-owned villages, censored political and social life—yet the mill people worked on, went to "preaching," spoke kindly of the mill-owner. Unions "weren't no good down there."

Unions had been tried. Thirty years ago the American Federation of Labor organized many villages, and got crushed in two years. During the world war Northern union money supported a string of strikes. In 1919-21, 50,000 operatives joined the

[1] August, 1929.

United Textile Workers, and dropped it like a hot cake when depression broke a big strike.

For the next few years the South thought it was on the way to solve the problem of industrial relationships without labor organization. Kindness flowed from employers. Sunday-school gospel gave the managers a glimpse of themselves as leaders of communities of brotherly love. Unions stood for the devil.

Meanwhile spindles poured Southward. The New England cotton industry had taken in its last dose of immigrant labor in 1914. Without the drug the present and the future were hard. But by moving to the South, where slavery had thrown a Black Belt about an Appalachian plateau full of Poor Whites, an artificial stimulus was to be had again.

Southern chambers of commerce made a big mistake. They advertised through the country that cheap, non-union, loyal labor, willing to work long hours a week, was to be had for the taking of a free factory site. Carolina's pride resented it. When manufacturers, using this labor, began to press it with speed-up systems, placidness was broken through. The result was the series of explosions that is taking place in the South now.

Since the first strike at Elizabethton five months ago, 150 branches of the United Textile Workers have been formed in Southern mill villages. The American Federation of Labor and the United Textile Workers have combined in raising a campaign fund by selling at a quarter-dollar apiece pins bearing a spinning wheel and a slogan "Organize the South." A staff of union agents is working in the textile districts. The venture is one of the biggest things in American labor history; it is a turning-point that may decide for one thing whether the textile industry can under American conditions dispense with trade unionism; for another, whether the doctrines of the American Federation of Labor mean enough in the American working-man's view of life to keep him organized under them; for yet another, whether the new South has so far left behind her slave-blighted past that she can come abreast of modern social standards.

The drive in the South coincides with a liberal attack on the old type of American trade unionism, and the South is now a battlefield between progressive and conservative unionism as well as between employers and mill people. The Communists who looked in for a couple of months have been scotched, but New York liberalism is quietly moulding the Southern unions into a body who may be looked to for a new lead in labor policy. Southern operatives do not feel the artificial division of their movement into economic and political fields that the American Federation of Labor has insisted upon. In one town they have just used a municipal election to sweep out the whole of a council that had supported strong-handed police methods. They may quite well do the same with State legislatures. The small white man's vote has been organized before, notably in South Carolina, where it was used to support the senator who in Washington protested, in defence of a high Southern tradition, against the countenance given in diplomatic circles to the brown-skinned representatives of the "nigger Republics of Central America." More liberal objects could have the same loyalty from Southern factory workers and farmers. But any labor party in the South would meet the same temptation to narrow racial legislation that has appeared in South Africa.

If the campaign plants a permanent movement in the South, as it gives every promise of doing, the effect on the cotton industry will be important. A year or two is long enough to allow for the coming of the 48-hour week, the passing of night work for women, and the closing of some of the gap between Northern and Southern mill wages. New England factories will be surer of their future. Mill-village paternalism will have achieved proof of its usefulness; it will have brought a backward people to a stage where they are capable of managing a movement of their own.

19. STRIKES DOWN SOUTH [1]

The people least surprised at the current strikes in the Southern textile industries must be the manufacturers. Whatever else they have or have not

[1] May, 1929.

been aware of, they have known for years that they were the beneficiaries of a differential advantage in long hours and low wages of their operatives. This distinction in cost of manufacturing cotton goods, falling chiefly upon the workers, for a long time did not excite comment, for three reasons, namely, (1) the operatives were newly transferred from agriculture where they had been ground down by a vicious credit system, and it was thought a boon that they should be receiving cash income; (2) harsh effects of low pay and long hours were mitigated, in appearance at least, by well-organized welfare work in the company-owned mill villages of the South; and, (3) the cotton manufacturing industry was regarded as a primary means of helping the South to its feet after the losses of the Civil War.

In the last five or six years, however, extraordinary changes have come in the textile industry, which have profoundly affected the complacency with which labor conditions in the South were viewed. The oldest seats of the industry, in New England and the Middle States, which not long ago did not take Southern competition seriously into account, have had the props knocked from under them. Southern manufacturers have invaded the field of the Northern mills by making finer and finer and more varied products. Competition of the artificial silks has entered to render the struggle between rival cotton manufacturers keener. The Northern mills have migrated Southward in one of the most conspicuous movements in the whole history of industry.

The South has invited this shift. Chambers of commerce, railroads, and power companies have advertised the advantages of Southern location, particularly in the matter of low wages, long hours, and absence of unions among the workers. The operatives have been pictured as plentiful, native American, loyal and submissive. Now this unabashed offering of the Southern Poor White to the textile manufacturer of the North and, indeed, of Europe, begins to dispel the reputation for charity, good will and patriotism which the Southern manufacturer had built up. The mask falls off, and the real features are recognized as bearing a startling resemblance to Capitalist Exploitation.

The day of this discovery had been held off by many devices, the least convincing of which was the assertion, made over and over again by employers and their representatives, that industry in the South would never show the characteristics which it has regularly developed elsewhere. The South, in spite of a profit motive which drove ahead at the expense of the worker, was going to hurdle the obstacles to economic peace which were familiar in other places and times. The reasons? Why, simple enough, it was asserted. The workers were all thoroughly reasonable Americans of old stock, and their employers were really more interested in turning out men and women than in producing yarn and cloth!

Anyone with the least acquaintance with industrial history knew that an average wage of $12.17 a week (census of 1925) and average full-time hours of 55.58 a week (1926) must either be steadily improved or must cause an upset. The 10- and 11-hour day and the 12-hour night (five nights a week) could not go much longer unchallenged by the workers themselves. Protest was precipitated in a series of strikes in Tennessee and the Carolinas beginning six weeks ago. The immediate demands are for higher wages and modification, perhaps abolition, of the new " stretch-out " system by which operatives are required to tend more machines. In the rayon factories of Elizabethton, Tennessee, the workers are newly transferred from a rural environment, and while their indignation has risen quickly, the fortunes of their revolt are guided by the moderate United Textile Workers. In Gastonia, North Carolina, and to a less extent elsewhere, the more advanced tactics of the National Textile Workers' Union have been able to whip jaded operatives, who have been in the mills for generations, into activity. It is interesting that only in the case of Gastonia has the demand for shorter hours (the 40-hour, five-day week in this instance) been made.

To date there is evidence of more violence on the part of the employers, or at least their sympathizers, than by the workers. Troops have been called out in Tennessee and North Carolina, but have had little to do.

The particular practices of employers which the workers want remedied are of less importance than the forces which were really responsible for bringing about the strikes, and these group themselves about the growing competition in the Southern textile field. Absorption of more and more of the Poor Whites into the factories, diminishing the numbers left on the tenant farms or up in the hills, was sure to increase the operatives' sense of independence. It does not matter that just prior to the strikes, on good report, there were more operatives seeking work than a year previous. The steady disappearance of the readily dislodged rural population was going slowly forward, and this gave the vast number which had been introduced into industry a greater feeling of security in voicing objections to the way in which their lives were being ordered.

Finally the worm turned. The seemingly fixed grin of the industrial Pollyannas has momentarily been changed to a frown, and eyes are opening wider. The grimace of the employers may turn to a gritting of the teeth, and the employes may fall short of their objectives or not gain them at all. But the fact will remain that the bedtime story of the goody-goody worker has lost its faculty of holding the attention. These strikes are compelling the South to recognize that it has opened its arms to capitalism, and that this means, so far as the worker is concerned, not the eternal crooning of a lullaby, but contending with a lusty infant who sometimes squirms and scratches.

Perhaps the door has been opened now to a new emergence of the Poor White. His original misfortune was in the killing competition of the black slave. The coming of the cotton factories in the South in the 'eighties gave him the opportunity of release from penurious staple agriculture. His own large numbers yet unindustrialized and his dire necessity made him tractable under labor conditions outgrown in the rest of America. But now that he is the hub about which so much industrial activity revolves, he suspects his importance, and will venture, oftener and oftener, to act upon his new consciousness.

Labor standards in the industrial South will be improved—by legislative enactment, by collective bargaining, by what will be given the appearance of voluntary action on the part of employers. Some day, not long from now, we shall be able to survey the fifty years which have turned the South from an exhausted agricultural region to the focus of manufacturing initiative and see that in tabloid and with remarkable compression it has repeated the experience of modern industry whenever and wherever it has taken hold. We shall not, as we are tempted to do now, think of the threat of this employer, the sluggishness or the venality of that legislature in turning down a child labor measure, or the criminal refusal of a labor leader to obey a particular injunction. We shall see that all of these, despite their degree of personal blame, have been primarily the inevitable functions of a fundamental economic change.

Every party to the present controversies must understand that the process will go on, not uninterrupted by accidental backsets and temporary false advantages, to a condition of prosperity founded upon fairness—a fairness maintained, however, by a balancing of powers between employer and employee, and not by professions of good will of manufacturer toward worker, professions rendered comic by the conspicuous submergence of the weaker partner.

III. CHILD LABOR

20. THE END OF CHILD LABOR [1]

The opinion of Judge Boyd, of the United States court for the western district of North Carolina, holding unconstitutional the child labor section of the war revenue bill, rouses insistent thoughts in the mind of a Southerner, with the conviction that the time is not too early to speak them. The temptation to find significance in the setting of the decision must be national. Opposition to the provisions of this " rider " to the revenue act, as to the similar requirements of the Keating-Owen bill, has been country-wide, it is true. And yet the men appearing before congressional committees against the measure of 1916 were Southern cotton manufacturers almost without exception. The fight was led by a former governor of North Carolina, and a solid block of witnesses came from that State.

Judge Boyd is the same man who held unconstitutional the original child labor act and, one day before it was to have gone into effect, issued a permanent order restraining its enforcement in his district. His decision was not closely followed by the Supreme Court in its affirmation which nullified the measure for the nation. It did not require a

[1] August, 1919.

three days' trial in the fall of 1917 to show who was most interested in that test case. Roland H. Dagenhart and his boys Reuben and John were poor operatives in a Charlotte cotton mill, but they were represented by counsel from New York and from two cities in North Carolina.

But these reflections are after all of minor consequence. A richer subject presents itself. In measuring the intensity of popular demand that children be taken out of mills and mines, in reviewing the testimony given to congressional committees and the sharply opposed majority and minority opinions of the Supreme Court on the Keating-Owen bill, and in viewing this latest phase of judicial negative, one is led to doubt the potency of legislature and bench in giving effect to the plain social and moral and economic needs of the people. One wonders whether a better force cannot, in this instance at least, be raised.

Testimony given to Senate and House committees by Southern cotton manufacturers and their attachés hostile to the Keating-Owen bill presented a complex of transparent evasions. It seems astonishing that men could be so artless in their side-steppings of the perfectly clear issue, and that they could drop into inevitable pitfalls without the least confusion. Every objection to the bill was urged more prominently than that which was uppermost in their minds. The absence of compulsory education that would absorb the energies of the liberated child workers, the necessity of industry to prevent moral perversion in persons of tender years, the importance to a child of the right to acquire while young the skill requisite to following the textile craft as a life's vocation, the robbing of widowed mothers of the means of a living through their boys and girls, the impropriety of factory inspection and the illegality of national interference with State affairs—all were put forward with more or less calm. An Alabama manufacturer met the challenge of a Pennsylvania congressman that the opponents of the bill did not dare argue in favor of the exploitation of children by avaricious industrial interests of the South, but contemptuously attacked the legislation by raising the hue and cry of constitutional infringements, by declaring to senators: "Gentlemen, I am one with sufficient audacity to attack this measure on its merits and solely on its merits. I feel that in this legislation we are attempting to infringe upon the inherent human rights of the poor young children of the South and everywhere else." The same man, refusing to look down the blind alley that confronts his child operatives, spoke truer than he knew when he said: "It seems to me that there is a point that should be entitled to your serious consideration—that in legislating out of the mills children under a certain age you are legislating them out at a time when they are most likely to become proficient in their chosen life's work. It has an important bearing on the child's outlook on life."

A plausible superintendent from the home of Cole Blease thought it would be "working a serious hardship on . . . these poor people—unfortunately poor people—not to allow them to make a nice living."

In answer to a question from a senator as to whether the opposition of the Cotton Manufacturers' Association of South Carolina was based on sympathy for the employes between the ages of 14 and 16, Captain Smyth, president of the organization and one of the oldest and most powerful cotton mill owners in the South, replied, " Our opposition is based upon a two-fold ground: First, you may say, because the age of 16 would cause a great hardship to a great many deserving people in South Carolina and in other Southern States; and secondly, we object to federal supervision and control of the industries of South Carolina." He declared it was a matter to be regulated by the State. Pressed to answer whether the thesis of the manufacturers lay in a constitutional objection, a legal objection, he replied, " Yes, sir; I am not a lawyer, and, of course, I do not express an opinion as to the constitutionality of it, but I do object to it as being an interference with our internal affairs."

A South Carolina superintendent, who was tripped in his specious assertion that in representing the Southern Textile Association, composed of " superintendents, overseers, mechanics, electricians, and . . . traveling salesmen handling mill supplies "

CHILD LABOR 221

(all of them naturally drawn to the side of the employers), he was also representing the common operatives, submitted that " if you discharge the children at the mills, or at any vocation, under 16 years of age, and let them loaf around on the streets, the morals of the children are going to be corrupted; there is no question about that, and for the good of the children and for the good of the people we ask you to be kind enough to leave us alone."

From this sort of representation of the children one turns in disgust. The compensating evidence and arguments of better champions before the committees (especially the doctrines of Dr. McKelway), the overwhelming passage of the bill by Congress, and the recruiting of an enforcement staff in the Children's Bureau under Grace Abbott, lent optimism with which to face Judge Boyd when he considered the Dagenhart case. Hopes dashed by his pitiably loose application of judicial acumen were further wasted in viewing the ponderous opinion of the Supreme Court.

The reasoning of the five justices of the majority and the four of the minority was diametrically opposed on the same few specific points. One not a lawyer cannot read the opinions without wondering whether his lay judgment, after all, is not in this case as good as that of the highest tribunal of the land. Thus Mr. Justice Day said for the five that " the thing intended to be accomplished by this statute is the denial of the facilities of interstate commerce to those manufacturers in the States who employ children within the prohibited ages. The act in its effect does not regulate transportation among the States but aims to standardize the ages at which children may be employed in mining and manufacturing within the States." On the contrary, Mr. Justice Holmes declared with equal emphasis for the four: " I should have thought that the most conspicuous decisions of this court had made it clear that the power to regulate commerce and other constitutional powers could not be cut down or qualified by the fact that it might interfere with the carrying out of the domestic policy of any State." The majority felt that the right to prohibit the movement of articles in interstate commerce rested upon the harmful character of such articles and, while eager to look back of the attempt to prohibit to affirm this basis of distinction in commodities, was not willing to discover a difference in making wholesome oleomargarine, and cotton cloth at the expense of children. This is precisely met by the minority, Mr. Justice Holmes arguing that " when interstate commerce is the matter to be regulated I cannot doubt that the regulations may prohibit any part of such commerce that Congress sees fit to forbid," and finding no difficulty in asserting that, " I should have thought that if we were to introduce our own moral conceptions where, in my opinion, they do not belong, this was preeminently a case for upholding the exercise of all its powers by the United States."

The case of Champion *vs.* Ames, quoted by the majority opinion as showing that the right to prohibit from interstate commerce is based on the character of the article excluded, is quoted by the minority to show how Congress may, in prosecution of a national policy, interfere legally with the internal affairs of a State. Further, there is a wide difference of judgment not only as to law but as to fact. The majority held the bill repugnant to the constitution because in regulating child labor within a State it meddled in " a purely local matter to which the federal authority does not extend." The minority, on the other hand, clearly found child labor a country-wide and not a local problem, declaring that " the national welfare as understood by Congress may require a different attitude within its sphere from that of some self-seeking State."

From this dispute one looks forward now to the decision of the Supreme Court of the United States upon the constitutionality of the child labor section of the revenue bill, not so much with nervousness or apprehension as with an inclination toward indifference. Learned citations of " Veazie Bank *vs.* Fenno, 8 Wall, 533, 19 L. ed. 482," " Flint *vs.* Stone Tracy Co., 220 U. S. 107, 55 L. ed. 389, 31 Sup. Ct. Rep. 342, Ann. Cas. 1912B, 1312," and " Hipolite Egg Co. *vs.* United States " with its lengthy reference merge with the shoddy testimony taken before congressional committees to give the person interested in the children the impression that in these researches he is treading upon fictions. His predisposition toward respect for legislative proceeding and obeisance before judicial dictum break down when he realizes that so far from affording remedies for the problem, they do not even deal with it in its substance. Just as the problem of child labor is one of flesh and blood, of alert minds or dull eyes, of dark-haired Mary and freckle-faced Billy, of the promise of youth and the duty of youth's fulfillment, so one wishes for a new program that can be grounded in the truth of the thing, which shall attain its ends by a reliance upon realities.

Much to the purpose here is a glance at the history of the cotton manufacturing industry of the South. The cotton gin and slavery saddled the Old South with agriculture. With some unimportant digressions, there was no departure from this course from the second decade of the last century until, say, 1880. By this year new factors had come into play. It was realized that exclusive attention to cotton cultivation had killed industry in the section, had precluded a diversified economic life. The Civil War bowled over the puppet of political salvation for the South, the induced belief that greatness lay in holding to outworn institutions through assertion of a theory of sovereignty. Reconstruction years, if they fanned a waning flame of sectional hatred in the minds of some Southerners, gave to a larger number a lesson which impressed the fundamental principle that the future of the South lay in work, in the humblest tasks of honest industry, in rational broadening of the economic order, in social coordination, in something like genuine democracy on the basis of contribution to the wealth and welfare of the people.

The manufacturing of cotton took the lead in the veritable boom which sprang from the deepest needs of the section and, aided by press and pulpit, spread through the South in the 'eighties, enlisting the enthusiasm of every town and opening to first view the possibilities of every country waterfall. The South was desperately poor, but there was faith in certain clear advantages for cotton manufacture which it was believed the section would enjoy. Cheap and abundant fuel, unused water powers, suitable climate, low cost of building materials, a home market for product, long days for long working hours, adaptable and supernumerous workpeople in the thousands of Poor Whites dispossessed by the slavery system and, most of all, proximity to the raw cotton, were urged upon investors in the new venture. There was no thought of exploiting the operatives. The man who erected a cotton mill was a public benefactor because he gave employment to men, women and children who sorely needed it; he believed himself a philanthropist and he was one. Everybody had to work—there was no room for social expediency. The opportunity for children to earn money in the mills was looked upon with public gratitude.

These superiorities of the South over New England were variously computed as totalling from 10 to 15 per cent. Some have proved more stable than others; one (that of proximity to the raw material) has in some instances proved even a disadvantage, strange as this may seem; but the history of the Southern industry has been preeminently one of development, and with development has gradually come disappearance or modification of the favoring differentials as compared with the North. Water powers have been bespoken and occupied, wood long ago ceased to be burned, a costly standard type of mill construction has taken the place of makeshift manufactories, the making of finer and finer goods has broadened the market to let in severe competition, the grouping of mills in certain centers has sometimes had the effect of driving the price of spot cotton above that prevailing in New York at the same time, hours have been steadily reduced. Once a good spinner ran eight " sides " of 56 spindles each, with 4000 revolutions of the spindle. Today a good spinner runs 10 or 12 sides of perhaps 108 spindles each, and at a speed of 10,000 revolutions. Then a man who ran five looms on plain two-harness sheeting was a skilled worker; now he runs 14 looms on the same goods. And so in every department of the business there has been an inevitable improvement and consequent leveling up toward the national standard.

With passing years more and more dependence for special advantage has been placed on the labor factor. As other superiorities of a more objective character have been neutralized by the very expansion of the industry, mill men have struggled ineffectually to maintain them and ended by nothing more substantial than regretting their passage. But they have held desperately to the labor differential. When hands became scarce in the 'nineties and preceding the panic of 1907, some cried for immigrants to take the places of those who had formerly been so freely obtainable from the farms, but some managers thought the cup could be drained still further. Better pay, more attractive economic conditions of work, inducement of great skill in the operatives were things not thought of, but instead agents were sent into the mountains to cart down the families pulled always with increasing trouble from the soil.

Since 1914, labor for the mills has been scarcer than ever. The Negro migration left vacancies, the army took its thousands, war construction held out unbelievable wage opportunities. The pay of the operatives began to jump forward in 10 per cent leaps. The manufacturers claimed that all of these advances were voluntary, but they were only superficially so. Underneath the increase was the unsatisfied demand for workers. Wage characteristics of previous periods recurred in more sharply defined form.

These promotions in pay afforded the first magnetism that drew the operatives together, and it is important to notice that this was an instrument born of their numerical deficiency, not of their conscious awakening to cohesion. Until the Armistice was signed, the growing, though still very incomplete unity of the workers (which had eventuated after 40 years in spite of a tradition of rural separation, low pay, disadvantageous proportion of women and children in the composition of the operative groups, and which began to transcend the segregation of the company-owned mill village), found itself given room for expansion in the more or less ready willingness of the mill managements to grant wage advances. When the fever of war work was abated, however, behold, a new thing presented itself. Assisted by the established national union of textile workers, the Southern operatives had made a beginning towards organization. The pressure of the unionized worker not finding itself answered by continued " voluntary " concessions by employers, led to strikes at Graniteville, South Carolina, at Columbus, Georgia, and other smaller mill centers.

A mill president of Columbus, addressing a group of superintendents gathered from the Southern States, described the situation with unconscious realism: " Now picture in your mind's eye, if possible, all of these cotton mill plants grouped in an immense valley under the Southern sun. Everybody happy—no one complaining—nothing is heard but the whir of machinery, the laughter of girls from window to window, or the song of the darkies as they unload the cotton at the mill platform. Everything looks happy and serene, does it not? Yes, but is it? God bless your souls, my hearers, it is in great danger! In danger of an intolerable invasion! Already being so invaded! You may not know it, but we here in Columbus know it!"

And the resolution to uphold the labor differential where others had failed found determined expression in the utterances of employers who abandoned evasions before Congress to speak economic archaisms to the capitalist South.

With no thought of inconsistency, the mill man just quoted declared organization of the workers would be stamped out by a closer union of the righteously indignant employers: "At the end of the war the cotton mills of the South will stand absolutely for their full legal right to operate that industry on the non-union basis. Closed non-union, if that will make it any stronger. Closed hermetically, climatically, sectionally, or any way you want it. Not only that. If necessary, a clarion call would go out and the 1070 textile plants of the South would form a unit, which in no uncertain terms would notify Messrs. Gompers, Golden and Company that they had better seek greener pastures, as they would simply be wasting their ' organization ' money in this part of the country.''

Other oratory showed how far yet the South has to go in industrial experience, how comparatively new is its development. Like an echo from the past comes this peroration: " The industrial South, as a whole, will never, while the country remains a republic, allow itself to be bound hand and foot, and virtually gagged politically, as is the industrial North today, by that thing which seeks to stab in the heart that inherent right of selective employment belonging to every individual, firm or corporation in this country. That unholy, foreign-born, un-American, socialistic, despotic thing known as *labor unionism.*''

The friend of the Southern cotton mill child knows that this man and those like him are not to be argued with, and relegates his blind obstinacy, with the tardy prescience of legislatures and exacting and faulty precedents of judges, to the background. In the rise of an economic consciousness in the operatives themselves he sees a hope that will not require even the passionate devotion of social reformers. An answer has come to those who would stretch the human patience where the physical advantage could not be extended; better than the assistance of child labor organizations, the enactments of Congress or the fiat of the Supreme Court is the challenge flung to the obdurate in the threat that, "Unless you yield we won't work!" It matters little that one great strike was lost by the operatives and that another was perhaps badly compromised. A blow has been struck. There has arrived that best help which proceeds not from without and that looks for no ulterior protection, but is self-help. It is the hair of the dog.

It was once thought that the Negro problem in the South devolved upon the shoulders of the liberating North; New England philanthropists established schools in the heart of the South, gave funds to churches and sent missionaries to the colored population. Then it came to be felt, slowly at first, that the Negro question was primarily a Southern one; Southern white men accepted positions of supervision over Negro education, and alumni of the University of Georgia did the field work for a government report on Negro schools. But now it begins to be sensed that perhaps, after all, to increase the self-respect and industry and efficiency of the colored population, it is best to rely upon the Negroes themselves; a Negro education society which a decade ago received from a white association ten dollars to accomplish its organization, has just raised among Negroes of the State $40,000 to carry on its work.

Sir Horace Plunkett viewed English attempts to solve the Irish question through political interference, and was persuaded instead in favor of agricultural cooperation at home. He wanted an economic remedy for an economic ill.

And so in the South with respect to the liberation of the children from the cotton factories. Employers' attempts to stem the tide will be of no avail. New England before this refused to learn from England's experience and tried to cling to child labor after it was doomed in public opinion and economic advancement. The South will go through the experience of England and New England if its chief men will not look the future in the face. Happily, there are many who not only acknowledge the facts but welcome them. These prefer to scrap spinning frames built low for child operatives rather than scrap the children.

The partial effectiveness of social propaganda and the unwillingness of courts to recognize that in such a matter they are made to be sanctions for the settled demand of the people, no longer matter. In unionism, the economic remedy for the economic evil has arrived.

21. THE SOUTH AND THE AMENDMENT [1]

Two things may be said about social-economic controversies: first, they are frequently nearest conclusion when the parties to them seem most widely

---

[1] January, 1925. It is fair to say that the Editor of the Manufacturers Record accompanied this article with hostile comment.

separated in points of view; second, solution usually comes through other forces than those appealed to by opposing sides.

Consider slavery: Calhoun whipped the South to a frenzy of defense at the very time the institution was showing unmistakable signs of decay. The South Carolinian took an old horse, galled and spavined and wind-broken, and, grinding rowels into his sides, rode him into battle as a charger. In the excitement of the time, the weakness of the mount did not show. Northern opponents accepted the terms of conflict. They were as blind to the impending doom of slavery as were Southerners. They believed that, unless desperate remedies sufficed, the poor old hack would mount their ramparts and pursue them for ever and a day.

Slavery was assaulted and supported on every ground oftener than on the economic. Calhoun and his school reared a whole separate political philosophy upon the exigency of slavery. Others scotched or attacked it on principles religious, moral, legal, historical and biological. Men tilted at windmills. They mistook the fiction for the fact. At the center of the complex was an economic perversion, and this was to prove controlling. Civil War or no Civil War, slavery had to die, because as an economic expedient it had reached the end of its tether.

Precisely the same comments hold with respect to child labor in the South and elsewhere in this country. Though controversy was never louder, it was never nearer its quietus. To continue my four-footed metaphor, hoofs are rattling into the home stretch, and that means the finish line is close ahead. Also, the question of the maintenance or prohibition of child labor will not be decided in accordance with the reasoning generally put forward. Battle cries in this instance are what they were in the slavery debate—federal domination, States' Rights, individual liberty, abstract justice, the presumption of exploiters. And now, as then, these are only surface evidences—they are the flows of lava down the sides of the volcano, while the central eruption is in the crater. Is it not possible for the South, without more waste of energy, to come to a calm view? If we would help toward rationality, we must analyze the Southern opposition to the Child Labor Amendment to the Constitution. Declaimants against this measure fall into two groups: the one is uninformed and, I think, sincere; the other is interested and, I am very sure, insincere. A different argument may be addressed to each group.

Those who honestly oppose the amendment do so, in the main, because they object to the "swollen federal authority" sprouting another "tentacle." They picture Congress as an octopus devouring the separate States. To these be it cautioned that there is an economic growth which refuses to be straightjacketed in political theory. As society makes progress in the arts of production, consumption and exchange, it means that the several parts of the economic body are becoming more specialized in their functions and, consequently, must be more closely interrelated. Bisect a man, and he cannot go on living in two parts, like a protozoan. The blood that vivifies every extremity must pass through a central heart. When America was thinly peopled and had few means of communication, colonies or States were separate principalities. Each was self-sufficient. Now all is changed, for each tiny community is dependent upon the whole country for its well-being. Federal administrative authority has had to expand to keep pace with economic trends. The federal government is not usurping State powers; rather, it is accepting responsibilities to which the State is proving itself unequal. Growing federal control is not a revolution, but an evolution in our public life.

The dishonest opponent of the Child Labor Amendment sets up justifications which sound plausible only so long as we do not examine them in the light of history. It is safe to say that there is not one argument against legislative control of child labor which is not both old and disproven. In the South, we forget two things—that we are not the first to face this issue, and that it will likely be decided for us as it has been decided for others. The Southern cotton manufacturer, in this particular, is repeating the history of the industry in England and New England. Lancashire mill masters fought the Factory Acts in protection of child workers 100 years ago in the same words as were used later in Massachusetts and Connecticut, and which roll off the tongues of Southern manufacturers today. Furthermore, most of the objections now being urged against federal regulation were urged but a few years ago against State regulation. In the recollection of the past, the most assertive brief for denial of legislative control rings hollow. The sovereign right of the State, the liberty of the individual, the unwisdom of child labor laws until we have compulsory school attendance, the freedom of contract, the good of widows and orphans—all are mockeries of the public confidence. All have gone down in defeat before this.

Cotton manufacture in the South began as an altruism. To judge from its typical arguments, now it has become a tyranny. This is a time for plain speaking. In a majority of instances, whether mill men will admit it or not, the welfare work in the villages is a device for delaying democracy. It is consciously maintained as a weapon against higher wages, shorter hours, greater independence of life of the operative. Paternalism, once absolutely necessary and for a long period enormously helpful, has had its day. The labor union, which so astonishes and outrages the Southern textile industry, is going to take the place of company government, and the company-owned town must give way before the steady march of incorporation.

The Northern mill is coming South. Competition will squeeze out and absorb the peculiar advantages heretofore enjoyed by the Southern cotton manufacturer, and with his old sectional profits will go his old sectional selfishness. As the industry grows in the South, it will not be possible for anybody to dominate the lives of the workers, for good or for bad, as it has been possible in the past. It is a question, in fact, whether federal legislation will not arrive upon the scene only in time to confirm what economic evolution has accomplished.

Just as was the case with slavery, child labor, at the moment it is most strenuously defended, is becoming obsolete. As a Southerner speaking to Southerners, I beg that we shall not, by opposing the inevitable, make a spectacle of ourselves.

IV. WELFARE WORK

22. COTTON MILLS IN SOUTHERN CIVILIZATION [1]

An exhibit of the present complexion of the Southern cotton mill village, no matter how detailed, is without meaning unless the setting is made clear; if the background is painted in faithfully, the foreground has so much the greater distinctness.

As in any momentous social change, the advance of the South from slavery and agriculture toward manufactures with free labor has brought its deplorable consequences. There have been negative elements in the calculus, and, too, absolutely hurtful practices backed by justifications sometimes ignorant and sometimes vicious. While special pleading cannot extenuate these, the compelling forward push of progress crowds them out and assigns them ultimately to the account of profit and loss.

In this belief the writer's purpose is to dwell upon positive accomplishments, without referring debit or credit to personalities, and seeking to count the net social gain. As a native Southerner, an honestly admiring student of its growing greatness, and one devoted to its interests, he wishes to be above all else helpful.

[1] January, 1924.

The human phase in the development of the cotton manufacturing industry in the Southern States stands out more importantly than any other. This is in spite of the fact that other features of the inception and advance of the mills have commanded the world's attention. In sixty years the South has gone far forward toward accomplishing an economic reformation. If at the outset the section could have foreseen all of the thousand directions in which prodigious enterprise must be put forward to achieve its task, it would perhaps have faltered in its purpose. As it happened, the immediate project was pressing, and men went blithely to work, meaning to utilize every opportunity that offered, and making opportunity where chance was unfavorable. The very fact of the attempt in large sense brought solution of the confronting problem—economic muscles strengthened with use.

After the Civil War and Reconstruction years, those in the South who had social imagination resolved to forget the hindrances of the past, and invited a new day. They began to make an Industrial Revolution. From whole absorption in agriculture, they focused the public mind on manufactures. In the midst of poverty, there was a will that found the way to capital investment in cotton mills. Few had had experience of the engineering problems involved, but factories sprang up and were equipped with the best machinery. With little initial knowledge of the relative advantages of water and steam power, judgment matured rapidly. Men who had never marketed anything but cotton, and that through routine channels, learned how to realize on manufactured goods. Planters who had drifted in the easy flow of agricultural existence discovered how to organize industrial undertakings, and fought upstream against competition.

But the change from the enslaved black hand guiding the plow to the free white hand assisting the spindle was the most novel of all the features of this new departure. The technical problems were difficult enough. The " Poor Whites " who entered the first mills had no industrial background. They had never seen frame or loom or speeder. Every process was awkward to them. Continuous hours of close attention to machinery contrasted with the variety and simplicity of old familiar habit in the country. They were not accustomed to coordination of effort, or to receiving directions. However, enveloping such perplexities were greater ones. In the main, the South's work had not been done for wages. Help had not been employed, but owned. The mills meant the arrival of the " cash nexus " with all its complications in store. The old economic controls of master over servant were relaxed, and a new way of joining the brains of management to the muscles of operatives had to be comprehended.

Further, the owners of factories and the workers in them had not been in partnership before. The

South's labor system had made them economic enemies. Every circumstance of the struggle for a living had been calculated to alienate them. The section held to the doctrine that it was cheaper to buy a man and maintain him than to hire a man and pay him. Those not offering to be purchased and not able to purchase others, were left out of the scheme of things. The plantation slaves pushed the Poor Whites out of economic participation. Had they possessed the means, most of them might have emigrated and left no great gap behind them. Remaining of necessity, they made places for themselves on the fringe of civilization and in most respects were just tolerated.

Slavery forbade the opening of opportunities to the unpropertied whites. Slave labor must be employed in simple operations, where gangs could be worked with small supervision of individuals, and in which the tasks, however hard, were slow and required strength and endurance rather than adaptability and intelligence. Thus enterprise expended itself in agriculture, and money sought investment nowhere else. The South believed dogmatically in the principle of the territorial division of labor—what a section fancies it can do best, let it do exclusively. Cotton was King, and interest in other activities than its cultivation was minor. Manufacturing, mining, and shipbuilding stood at a minimum. Fabricated goods came from the North and from Europe. The simplest appurtenances of agriculture itself were purchased from a great distance. Able to buy from others, the South did not trouble to make for herself, and took distinct pride in being a society of landed gentlemen despising "truck and barter." Few cities grew, and fewer sprang up. Life was lived too largely in splendid isolation on planters' estates. If there was social intercourse, it was because gentle-folk had much leisure to devise means of seeing each other, if, indeed, they were not absentee landlords enjoying winter seats in the capitals.

All this meant that the Poor Whites not only had no place provided for them by those in social control, but could not make room for themselves in any fashion to give them a future. If little mills and forges existed here and there, they were often worked by slaves. Industrial communities held out many chances of a living to tradesmen, common laborers, mechanics and small neighboring farmers. In the absence of these, there were few to constitute a middle class. Gentlemen planters were often their own merchants and brokers, while many functions now performed by business men then belonged to the profession of the law; lawyers consummated land deals and acted as trustees and investment bankers. Artisans were frowned upon, for these did not fit into the South's "peculiar institution," refusing to buy slaves and demanding respect for free labor.

The Poor Whites must live, then, on the land. The South believed in the cultivation of staple crops—

cotton, rice, tobacco, and sugar. The plantation régime must be as nearly as possible automatic. Experiments in farming were not popular and not profitable. The Negroes, at best substituting mere duty for ambition and obedience for understanding, were not original workmen themselves, and enslaved the mind of the master. He became as unperceiving as they, and the masters being the only part of the population that counted, the whole South was cast into bondage. The section went on making more and more cotton, exploiting itself blindly and making sterile its own social inventiveness as persistently as it killed the fertility of its soils. Finally, habit became principle, and an unlucky agricultural twist was erected into a total political and economic creed.

The whole credit mechanism was founded on cotton cultivation. Farmers who needed to have store goods and equipment advanced to them had to raise cotton if they wanted to be trusted. It was the sure money crop. Thus for the Poor Whites life on the land must be somehow in the service of cotton if they chose to remain in the districts where the staple grew. A few of them could work as overseers, but the rest must be tenants on mean conditions. Some barren land there was in the low hills between coastal plain and fall river line, and here many clung on as squatters. The Poor Whites who were not meager retainers of the plantation masters lived in the farther uplands. Here, to be sure, there was not the competition of the slave on every hand, but the soil did not lend itself to cultivation readily, and produce must be carried to distant markets over intolerably bad roads. The mountaineers held desperately to such of the free traditions implanted by German and Scotch-Irish forbears as had not been obliterated by the slave system of the country, but a sensitive personal pride living on in the face of reducing poverty was all that was left.

Walter Page knew the Poor White, and called him "the forgotten man." He was dispossessed. Such public education as existed was charity, and very insufficient charity at that. The only teachers of the Poor Whites were preachers and politicians, and these played equally upon the emotions with equally hurtful results. The church could offer only patient piety under affliction, and the politician dispensed civic quackery. Because of economic displacement the Poor White hated the Negro and, always ready to respond to any call of race prejudice, voted with the planter, though the economic interests of the two parties of white men were as separate as the poles.

Frederick Law Olmsted went through the South in the decade before the Civil War, and saw it as it was. Little that was good or bad escaped him. He summed up his observation of Virginians in words that applied to the whole section: "It is the old, fettered, barbarian labor-system, in connection with which they have been brought up, against which all their enterprise must struggle, and with the chains of which all their ambition must be bound. This conviction . . . is forced upon one more strongly than it is possible to make you comprehend by a mere statement of isolated facts. You could as well convey an idea of the effect of mist on a landscape, by enumerating the number of particles of vapor that obscure it.'' The Poor Whites were bondmen beyond everyone else in the South, for the masters, however cramped their outlook, were at least in possession, and the slaves, however little their liberty, were at least secure. The unpropertied whites had no place in the community.

Nor did the Civil War and emancipation of the slaves help matters for the outcasts. They came back from serving the South in the armies to find that there was no more place for them to serve at home than before. The Negro had been freed politically, as the North supposed, but he was economically as much a slave as ever—as dependent upon the white man of property and position. In the main he did his old work, and thrust the Poor White aside as he had always done. The stricken condition of the section rendered chronic misfortune doubly galling. Here and there, it is true, in the breakup of a plantation some one of the tenant class entered upon the purchase of land, and through Reconstruction years every white vote was rallied against the Carpet Bagger and his black following, which somewhat increased all the whites' understanding of each other.

For the fifteen years following the war all was political hatred, economic confusion, sectional animosity and human hopelessness. But finally, about 1880, the South turned over a new leaf. The section forgot old tenets and formed a new faith. This was that the South must cease thinking of herself as peculiar in economic as well as in political character, and must follow those pursuits which the rest of the country found profitable. The cry was: " Bring the cotton mill to the cotton field! " Cities which had previously forbidden the use of the steam engine within their limits, little towns which had been stagnant and despondent, and even country neighborhoods took up the shout and rapidly made plans for manufacturing the staple. Any man of leadership or promising business connections might be forced to the front. Planters, merchants, doctors, teachers, lawyers, and even preachers headed factory enterprises. The last patriotic dollar that the local community or the people of the State at large could muster was summoned to set the project going, and intending Southern manufacturers posted North to enlist the monetary aid and industrial experience of commission houses and machinery makers.

One of the chief reasons for building cotton mills was the purpose of their projectors to furnish employment to the Poor Whites. One is tempted to believe profits a greater incentive than philanthropy. However that may be in general, the South was in strange circumstances, and novel motives in business showed themselves. Full explanation lies in many facts, but the chief is that the people still looked to the old leaders for help and direction, and these ex-slaveholders and ex-Confederate officers simply played familiar rôles under unfamiliar conditions. It is true that the new manufactures would draw money into the South and put it in circulation, thus quickening business in every department, but really nothing can alter the fact that scores of men built factories as much from altruism as from any other cause. No one can understand the history of the Southern mill operative or appreciate the significance of his present position in relation to his employer and the public life unless realizing that the old South was metamorphosed into the new. In the Middle Ages, the landlord was responsible for all the interests of the people on his manor; in the same way the master craftsman in the town assumed responsibility for his apprentices. It was inevitable that the Southern man of affairs, who had once controlled destinies as of right, should, flung into a new situation, offer to do so as a matter of duty. It is impossible to change an ingrained social habit overnight, and, happily, it is equally unwise to do so. A principal point about the South's industrial awakening in the 'eighties is that she accomplished it herself, though enlisting, it is true, the quick assistance of outsiders commercially interested. Even those founders of mills who wished to take advantage of a ready and cheap labor supply, were conscious that industrial progress, no matter if promoted with money-making as the direct motive, was yet the most wholesome school of social advancement for the South; they knew that their very selfishness was inevitably generous.

Of those who turned philanthropist-manufacturers it was said: "Probably no better field for the exercise of such motives could be found than among the large planters of the South. Long accustomed to leadership in all the political, business and social affairs of the community, imbued with a spirit of helpfulness which their control over the . . . earthly destinies of others taught them to exercise during slavery days, taught finally by their own discouragements during the years of reconstruction how bitter is the curse of poverty, these men would not lack . . . the willingness to help their poorer neighbors along the road to . . . industrial independence." And another who knew his own people declared that the spirit inherited from the ante bellum South " has maintained . . . the old sense of responsibility toward the unprivileged," that it is this " quick sense of social obligation," this " local conscience " which has given " distinction and beauty to the allegiance between the aristocracy and the common people." Anyone who observes the solicitude of Southern cotton manufacturers for the welfare of their villages realizes the truth of Mr. Page's remark respecting the people of the section, that " they are not only demonstrative; they really care for one another in the most affectionate ways. Helpfulness is not an act of conscience; it is an impulse."

Nothing that has been done in welfare work in the Southern cotton mill villages in the last forty years is new in spirit or in main outline. Robert Owen at New Lanark, Scotland, a century and a quarter ago inaugurated " an institution for the formation of character," a community kitchen, a model school, outdoor games and a band. William Gregg at Graniteville, South Carolina, 75 years ago rightly called his village " an asylum for widows and orphans," and considered himself a social missionary.

The motive of human helpfulness is illustrated by the building of the Salisbury Cotton Mills. The town in 1887 had not retrieved the losses the war cost, nor had it tried to do so. An interdenominational protracted meeting was held with the unexpected result that the preacher soon began to advocate a cotton mill as the best means of salvation for the community. It was useless to urge industriousness upon sodden, hopeless people so long as there was no opportunity of employment. The town caught the new religion, and it was a group of ministers and leading church members who projected the manufacturing enterprise. A population which had been poor and ignorant and lazy soon became thrifty and prosperous, with the consequence that the moral problems of the town solved themselves. The Charleston Manufacturing Company half a decade earlier was commenced with the philanthropic incentive prominent in the minds of investors, and Clinton, in the same state, exhibited the same feeling.

The great morality in the South then was to give the Poor Whites a chance to make a living. Their crying need was to be welcomed back into economic citizenship. Their history in the mills from 1880 until today has been the progress of that re-entry. Perhaps the way chosen was tortuous, implying the maximum of readjustment on the part of employers as well as workers. Certainly it has involved hardships, and almost two full generations of operatives have, whether knowing it or not, given their lives toward a consummation devoutly to be wished. But it has been the only possible solution. No amount of scheming could have brought the South into social health so long as agriculture was the sole dependence of the people. The institution of slavery had worked a contortion of the body politic which would not yield to religious or political or educational massaging, but which required painful corrective exercises. Manufactures combined with agriculture gave an alternate employment, brought money into the section through the sale of finished product, raised the price of cotton in local markets, increased land values, bettered roads, diverted attention from the eternal question of the Negro and discredited the politics which lived only upon this issue, and, altogether, swept the South nearer to main national currents of thought and action.

In the first mills hours were long, pay was little, and a large proportion of children was employed. Almost 25 per cent of the operatives in Southern mills in 1880 were children, as compared with half this percentage in the mills of New England. This was not a hardship, but a boon. There was no complaint of exploitation. Masters were as hard pressed as men, and all struggled to hold on to the means of livelihood. Of these years it has been said "There was no thought . . . with regard to who should work or how many hours they should work. The problem was not one of seeking or creating wealth; it was essentially one of employment, of human welfare in the sense of providing instrumentalities by the use of which men, women and children could earn. . . . The exigent demand for the bare necessaries of life, which could be gotten in the cotton mills of that period only by the combined toil of the whole family, overshadowed all other considerations. Literally it was a question of 'bread and meat,' and the mills provided for thousands who could not otherwise subsist."

When it was known that a factory was to be erected, mountaineers and poor tenants began to inquire eagerly for employment, and to make plans for moving their families to the new village. When the mill was placed in operation others came in ready scores. One is reminded of the way in which poor men were anxious, in the Middle Ages, to occupy cottages in the shadow of a protecting castle. When times are troubled, whatever the period of history, the weak become attached to those with greater strength. The mills provided everything, for they built industrial communities in open cotton fields, or cleared away forests to secure places by water power. Homes, stores, schools, churches—all were the gifts of the management, for there was no other to give.

It is not hard to picture the life of the Poor Whites before they came to the factories. It was simply the reverse in every respect of the life of the planters, who nourished an unnatural culture and acquired unlucky wealth by a false labor system. More eloquent than any spoken account of the Poor Whites is the telling silence of most of the writing of the period concerning them. They had been left out of the calculation until the doors of cotton mills were opened to them.

Those who have remained on the tenant farms or persisted in the mountain hollows show today a condition not different from that obtaining 45 years ago. If we contrast those who have been left in the old environments with those who changed their whole habit of life by going to the mill villages, we get the clearest idea of just what has been accomplished.

Just last year a thorough investigation was made of the social status of white tenants in two townships of Chatham, a mid-state county in North Carolina, and the results, making a vivid close-up picture, were published by the State University. Had the survey been made half a century earlier, the findings would have been much the same. This district before the War was a typical seat of slavery. Except for a small cotton mill, there are no villages in the area, the houses being only three to the square mile. " The cash in circulation in the homes of the 51 white tenants was only 12 cents a day per person. . . . Here certainly is life reduced to its very lowest terms in money." In the white cropper families, indeed, there was only eight cents daily cash per person. A large part of the little they raise is for consumption then and there; the crops sold for money scarcely count. The stores advance supplies and so do the landlords, and the debts thus incurred eat up most of what salable crops might bring. White cropper families receive on the average only $153 yer year in money, and most of this comes at the end of the year. The report declares: " There is too little ready cash in circulation in the country districts of North Carolina and too little accumulated wealth. Until both are multiplied many times over, the 1,200,000 farm people of North Carolina are a mired wheel in our civilization."

In these townships the black tenants are actually ahead of the white—the Negro cropper families get $197 per year in cash as against $153 for the white. The whites' " standards of living are higher but their levels of life are lower than those of the black farmers alongside whom they live and work, inevitably so because their average cash income is less—22 per cent less than that of the black croppers, 47 per cent less than that of the black renters, and 74 per cent less than that of the black owners." It is pertinently asked, " Can a civilization forever endure on the basis of political freedom and economic serfdom? "

Of the dwellings of the white renters in this district it is reported that " 20 have 203 window lights out and 10 have shutters off. In more than half of these dwellings it is possible to study astronomy through the holes in the roof and geology through the cracks in the floor." Such sanitary provisions as exist are negligible or constitute an actual menace in each case. The tenant families paid on an average $48.64 in the year to doctors and druggists. " Nearly one-ninth of the total cash incomes . . . went for illness, to say nothing of the funeral expenses when the illness ended in death." In one home the doctor's bill was $400 and the total wordly goods of the tenant $289. " Death is more endurable than sickness in many tenant houses." Forty-seven out of 148 children borne by the mothers in these homes are dead. Not one of the 178 members of these households has ever been vaccinated. Almost no printed literature of the State on health and housekeeping and farming reaches their homes.

Such a community can have few facilities making for fullness of life. It is rightly observed that the opposition of such a population to taxes is the opposition of the collapsed pocket-book. "All the elementary schools in the open country are housed in buildings that are old and weather-stained. None of them have been built within the last twenty years. They are taught for the most part by young girls in their 'teens. . . ." The illiteracy percentage among these tenants is 9.2. "For nearly exactly half of the renter households, school culture may be said to stop on a fifth reader level. . . . For nine-tenths of the cropper families life stops on a fourth reader level." No member of any one of these tenant families ever went to college.

Books and papers and magazines play the smallest possible part in these homes. No families borrow volumes from any school or other public library, and two have no books except the Bible. The scattered churches are the most active centers of community life, and these are broken reeds on which to lean. All but two of the preachers serving the eight churches are non-residents of the locality. Seven of the churches have preaching only once a month. Nearly a third of the white cropper families are "habitually absent from church. No way to go, church too far away, no clothes, they say." Furthermore, they are too proud to go to church when they have nothing to put into the collection box.

Many families had no part in the life of the community, rarely leaving their own rented acres. No family went to a circus and only one to a moving picture show in the year.

It is concluded that few of the white croppers are capable of being helped into farm ownership, and the croppers constitute one-fourth of all the white tenants in this district and in the South. It is believed that only 2800 of the 32,000 white tenants in North Carolina possess the qualities that would make for success even were the way to land proprietorship opened to them by government grant or otherwise.

It is stated that more than a third of the people in the townships of Chatham County surveyed have moved out in the course of a generation. It is safe to say that most of these have gone to cotton mill villages. Their lives in their new communities present a contrast to the old state of existence at a minimum.

It must be remembered in viewing the variety of social facilities offered by the mills that most of the textile plants which have risen in the South have involved the building of villages. If the factories have not been located in the open country, the towns near which they were placed possessed no housing room for a sudden influx of population. In most instances the cotton mill communities have been made out of hand. Every department of life of the workers had to be supplied outright or indirectly provided for by the managements.

The best education in the South today is training in the elements of civilization. The whole industrial village is a vastly more important school than the particular building in which classes are held. Programs for rural advancement, promising as these are, cannot be as immediately successful as the influences emanating from an industrial undertaking. In the country families are scattered, and separation makes for ignorance and retards collective action. In the mill towns social work is at close range. Improvement in the standard of life does not depend upon poor acres poorly cultivated; it is not necessary to reform a stubborn agricultural tradition in order to render home and neighborhood environment more grateful. In the mill villages the manufacturing plant (in the industrial history of the South, luckily, almost constantly active) is offering steady work constructively directed and producing regular cash wages. The people have been lifted bodily out of many of their old hindrances, and a minimum of negative work need be expended in order to engage their best capacities.

The chief social agencies in the village are the mill itself, the home, the church (often, in contrast to the country, a union church), the school, the Christian Association and the welfare department. There are instances in which some of these are absent altogether or are not functioning fully, perhaps because the mill does not have its own village or the plant is a very small one. However, in the textile communities as a whole, welfare work is being more and more widely extended, its ramifications are becoming greater and its methods are maturing. There is no other industry in the United States which directly undertakes so much for the social improvement and well-being of its workers as the cotton manufactures of the South.

A teacher in a leading mill town has put the matter simply: "The man on the job is the vital factor in our textile industry. Money will buy the most modern machinery, provide the best material equipment, furnish raw material for manufacture, fill the pay envelope; but machinery, equipment, raw material, pay envelopes, while important factors in the product of industry, are reduced to zero if the human factor, the man on the job, is a zero factor. These obvious facts present our obvious need, better . . . help. The . . . question, 'How will we get it?' is answered by the . . . reply, 'Train it.'"

It is generally admitted and even declared by Southern cotton manufacturers that their village welfare work is maintained because it pays in dollars and cents to have alert, intelligent, healthy operatives who are happy in their homes and get as nearly as possible maximum production from the machines they tend. At the outset of the cotton mill era in the South this was not so true; the motive of kindliness for its own sake operated more largely because the workers needed it more and the far looser competition of those days had not bred up the same commercial responses in the manufacturers which are active now. One who speaks for the industry has compressed the truth into one sentence: "As a matter of fact this whole proposition of social advancement is largely based on business, not philanthropy, although some of the leaders, after years of effort, become so greatly interested in the results they are obtaining that they would deeply resent a statement that their prime motive in undertaking all this work was to prevent labor turnover and thus secure a greater quantity of a better quality of product."

The point should be made that no matter what the stimulus to welfare work in the villages, whether that of business efficiency or of engaging social experimentation, the results in social betterment, so far as 193,000 cotton mill operatives of the South are concerned, stand the same. If managements embrace such a program as a part of their money-making enterprise, it is likely to be pushed so much the more actively. It is true that welfare work was expanded during recent war years partly in the purpose to escape excess profits taxes by including as much as possible under the head of expenses, and partly because competition for workers was keener than before and the more attractive a village the better its chances to secure and hold operatives. But, again, motives do not matter. It is even said by some mill men who are perfectly in the councils of the industry that "manufacturers have frequently, and ... for the most part, in reality opposed improved conditions. They did not have time to think them out and bother about them, but on general principles they objected to any present expense, or ' by giving sweetmeats to the poor, to teach them wants they never knew before.' " Whatever their disinclinations, however, these employers have been dragged along in the procession and have had to live up as best they could to the standard set by progressive companies; otherwise they would have had high turnover in an inefficient labor force.

All the agencies of the mill community may be made to work together for a given end. They are often focused on the children because more teachable. This is fortunate, too, because they will make the next generation very different from the present one. The problem of 150 malnourished children in one mill village is a case in point. It was attacked as follows: by teaching all the children of the village in school the cause of malnutrition and the remedies for it; by special classes for malnourished children taught by the community nurse; by visits to the homes and conferences with mothers at which directions were given by doctor and nurse; by the affected children keeping diet cards checked by the nurse; by instruction of the children in the domestic science department of the school in the preparation of prescribed food; by the preachers in their sermons urging care of the body; by the mill providing cow-pastures and stalls, and encouraging the production of milk and butter. The result was that only 14 of the 150 remained as much as five pounds under weight, and these were hampered by some physical defect which was treated. The superintendent of a large plant said that he worried as much about the cow-sheds in the village as about the machinery in the mill. Some companies extend financial facilities to their operatives to enable them to own cows, and supply dipping vats the use of which is compulsory.

Schools in villages owned by mills are erected by the companies, salaries of teachers are shared by company and county, and school terms are generally longer and quality of instruction better than in the adjacent districts. Even where the mills circle thriving cities, it is possible for the villages to have made greater relative progress in recent years than the municipality. The formation of a new school district by 12 mill villages and two suburban communities just outside Greenville, South Carolina, is an illustration in this connection. This district has 12 grammar schools, two high schools and a rural school, and is erecting new buildings. There will be a library of some 4000 volumes in addition to the separate school libraries, and books will be distributed by automobile truck, their use thus being rendered inviting.

The progress of individual schools is illustrative. At Pacolet the first teaching was done in the basement of a church. Three or four teachers instructed between 200 and 300 pupils in 10 grades. This was in 1896. In 1915 and 1918 eight additional class rooms were provided. Now a new plant costing $125,000 has 19 rooms and an auditorium, and there are 18 teachers covering eight grades in which 425 pupils are enrolled. There is a domestic science laboratory where cooking is taught with the aid of the best equipment, and a domestic arts laboratory given to sewing instruction. Besides a complete outdoor playground, there is an indoor playroom with shower baths in connection. There is a manual training department, the library has 1000 volumes, and the building houses a part time vocational school for children working half the day in the mills, and also conducts an evening school for adults. Music appreciation is given in all grades. At Piedmont the first school, in 1877, had one room and one teacher. By 1880 there were five teachers and 175 pupils working in new buildings. By 1890 the grades taught were six. Average attendance was poor. In 1920 a new building was erected at a cost of $100,000, and there are now in the school 21 teachers and over 700 pupils. Average attendance last year was 80 per cent. There is a science laboratory. An increase of 30 students in the high school this year is mainly due to local pupils' remaining longer in school.

The mills in some instances have vacation camps for the villagers. All with any pretence of welfare work have athletic grounds and many have gymnasiums and swimming pools. The newer villages are apt to have cottages planned in skillful variety, with winding instead of straight streets, and everywhere vegetable gardens and flower beds are encouraged. Houses rent regularly for 25 cents per room per week, and, plastered and equipped with electricity, are ten times better than the homes that most of their occupants came from in the country. Stores in the mill villages sell at reasonable prices and do not allow their patrons to become engulfed in debt by a vicious credit system as is the case in rural districts—the stores are dependent upon the people, not the people upon the stores. Besides the large item of house-rent, wages are to a considerable degree paid in kind, as in free wood, coal at or actually below wholesale prices, free gardens and seeds and pasturage, unpaid attendance by physician, dentist and nurse and welfare facilities generally.

Mr. Frank Tannenbaum in a recent article has quoted Mr. Stuart Cramer to the effect that the Southern cotton manufacturer has perhaps one-third of his capital tied up in a village with all its appurtenances, whereas his Northern competitor has every dollar of his capital invested in producing equipment. It is declared that the Southern mill man would be glad to get rid of his village. As a matter of fact, in the present condition of the South, the mill village is as much a part of the producing machinery of the plant as are the spinning frames and looms themselves. The South enjoys advantages in cotton manufacturing over the North and Middle States which permit heavy investment in villages with profit still accruing, as is evidenced by the coming south of Northern textile firms which adopt the local custom. So long, moreover, as workers continue to be drawn fresh from rural districts, without industrial tradition and lacking the habit of community life, the villages are as helpful as they are necessary in bridging an economic gap.

When one contrasts the poverty of life on tenant farms or in mountain regions with the equipment of civilization which the mill villages hold out, he appreciates the social advantages which these industrial communities have been to the South. They constitute a benevolent despotism without doubt, but one must always remember that the South is in transition from a stultifying single pursuit of agriculture to a livening and health-giving fusion of manufactures with farming. If this experiment is to be successful, there must be economic tutelage of the working population which is altering occupations so violently. In Russia the Bolshevists have declared frankly that their autocracy is intended, that there must be strong leaders to assume responsibility if the new social venture is to carry through. Only by such means can the democracy aimed at materialize.

And the same is true in the South. A people who had no part in the life of the section are being brought back into its work and councils and, being the producers, they will one day control its destinies. Much may be said of the drawbacks involved in the unincorporated company town in the South, but the indictment is softened if it is seen that it is a feature of the economic adolescence of the section, for all adolescence tends to present values out of proportion, and breeds impatience, selfishness, uncalculating enthusiasm, over- and under-confidence. All in all, it is justly said that " the social conditions of the mill operatives . . . have improved during the last 25 years as rapidly as the operatives could adapt themselves to them." In any event, the judgment of the observer of their history a generation from now will be that, whatever their advantages or detractions as viewed from this instant angle or that, the mill villages were a natural and necessary stage in industrial upbuilding.

Mr. Tannenbaum has concluded that the South is burying its Anglo-Saxons in social stagnation and positive economic repression. For example: " These people are being denuded, stripped, washed out, destroyed. They are being reduced to a state of childish impotence where they have to be taken care of and where they produce nothing. They give the South no poets, no artists, no politicians [Heaven be praised!], no orators, no teachers, no business men, no men of adventure, no builders, no engineers, no technicians, no leaders in any field of activity whatever. So far as the community is concerned, they might as well never have been at all." And he thinks further: " One gets the feeling when he sees these long, emaciated figures, wan and sleepy-looking and without any vividness or interest, that it were far better had they remained on the farm and scratched the soil with their nails. It were far better that they had starved on bitter roots, killed one another in long family feuds, that their children had lived in ignorance and had gone bare-footed, ridden horses bareback and hunted wildcats, some going to the madhouse, some making moonshine, some escaping . . . into a mountain or valley school. . . . The adventure of living was not at an end."

While there is much to tempt the immediate observer to this view, the economic historian finds the matter different. It is not true that " the mountaineer or small cotton farmer who moves to the mill village is lost to the community." It is his introduction to the community. It is not better for his children to hunt wildcats and grow up moonshiners than to be set physically and mentally right and afterwards make yarn and cloth. Mr. Tannenbaum misconceives life on tenant acres or upland hillsides to be an adventure. It possesses its own emphatic qualities of serfdom. The plan of life it represents has been tried, and has brought the South nothing. It is probable that the proportion of outstanding individuals coming from the mill villages has been as great, in an equivalent period, as the number coming from the Poor Whites in their old state. If one considers only the mill superintendents and presidents who have risen from operatives, this is patent. But it is more important to understand that what the South requires now is not spectacular figures. Of these it has boasted too many to its hurt. What it needs is a thrifty, cash-earning, school-going, health-conserving, industrial population, and the cotton mill operative in his thousands is conferring the most patriotic service upon his community and country.

The mill villages are not only an escape from the economic anæmia of rural lapse, but they are sure to be a door to wider participation. It is not gratuitous to suggest in a spirit of friendliness what an ever greater number of mill men are coming to see, namely, that there are signs current in the mill villages of growth into a new order. That man is most out of accord with his own time who does not sense that it holds in itself the seeds of change.

Southern cotton manufacturers, consciously and by force of circumstances, have possessed the character of economic statesmanship, and it is this same responsibility which one appeals to when he speaks of alterations which the future is likely to bring. Unless the best that has been accomplished by these men in the past has been totally mercenary and on other counts grudging, next steps in social evolution in the South will find the accustomed leaders adaptable and intelligent.

Pure paternalism, once necessary, is being modified and managements are finding that facilities, such as the use of welfare buildings, may in great part be paid for by the operatives enjoying them, with lightened burden to the company and increased interest on the part of workers. As this tendency develops, wages, now greatly supplemented by the bounty of the mills in a variety of services and subsidies from church to moving picture, will incline to be paid more and more completely in money. There are manufacturers who conduct no welfare work in their villages directly, but encourage improvement organizations of the operatives themselves as a substitute. Others feel definitely that as the first boon conferred by the mills was the bringing of families from isolation and poverty into community living where they could earn, so the next desirable step is to relate the operative to the general body of the citizenship. The way is being paved for this by two tendencies; first, the fact that the operatives' station is no longer looked down upon by the rest of the white people as it was twenty-five years ago, and second, that growing manufacturing establishments with all the activities incident to community life cannot remain indefinitely near a town without incorporation to it or, if the mill villages are in sufficient number, without important forms of cooperation between the mills themselves, which, in course of time, will work toward the same result. The Parker School District outside of Greenville is a case in point. Some manufacturers are glad their plants are located in towns. They prefer paying taxes to the municipal corporation and relying upon civic enterprise in educational and welfare matters.

The South, from a discouraged start forty-five years ago, is soon to be the chief seat of the cotton manufacturing industry of this country. New England is steadily losing ground in the race. Between 1904 and 1919 every State with a million or more active spindles lost in the percentage of its spindles to those of the whole country except South Carolina, North Carolina, Georgia and Alabama. Massachusetts, Rhode Island, New Hampshire, Connecticut and Maine lost. In the same period, while New England and the Middle Atlantic States together lost 11 mills, the South Atlantic and South Central States gained 53. The census which once needed to pay no attention to the Southern industry and later gave it somewhat grudging reference, has narrowed praise of New England to a single State and reports a new statistical alliance in the fact that in 1919 more than half of the total value of cotton manufactures came from Massachusetts and the Carolinas. Between 1914 and 1919 the percentage of workers employed by corporations in all descriptions of manufactures increased faster in the South than in the rest of the country. Thus management is rapidly being standardized. In percentage of increase of fine goods, which may be held to reveal more than any other one item, the cotton-growing States, between 1914 and 1919, had a score of 72.5, while New England registered a positive loss of 8.8. In the same period, while New England in the pounds of its yarn for its own consumption fell from 98 to 84 millions, the cotton-growing States rose from 12 to 14 millions; in respect to yarn produced for sale, New England gained two millions while the cotton growing States gained 16.

As mills increase under Southern enterprise and Northern firms come south, competition for labor will be closer. Alternate occupations to that of cotton manufacturing will present themselves, and the phrase " once an operative, always an operative " will lose its meaning. The South will find it more and more difficult and be less and less prompted to cling to forced industrial differentials hitherto prevailing. The question will cease to be one of lessening distinction between sections, and will become one of the new industrial level to be reached in the South when her textile opportunities will be more completely occupied.

The South has long been approaching national standards. As she comes into national preeminence, the error of child labor will disappear and, whether through evolution of shop committees or organization into trade unions, workers will assume responsibility for their economic and social lives.

V. THE OLD SOUTH AND THE NEW

23. THE ECONOMIST LOOKS AT RELIGION [1]

Recently I revisited, after an absence of twenty-five years, a country neighborhood in Virginia with which I was familiar as a child. The family which I knew best had moved away, and their house, now in the hands of impoverished cousins, was falling into decay. Other landmarks along the road were missing. I finally made out that a cowshed comprised a part of another house I had known. A small settlement of Negro cabins had disappeared with the exception of one shack with roof fallen in on a broken ridgepole. Fields that had been tilled were grown up in broomsedge and scrub-oak.

Only the road was the same. Its mud holes were in the old places. Its bridges spanned the same gullies, though these were washed wider.

I pushed open the door of the little church. It was silent and empty except for green flies bobbing against the windows. The same little gasping organ was in its place, with dusty paper flowers on top of it. On the pulpit was a pile of Sunday school quarterlies, with the identical lessons I had studied— Elisha with his bears set upon scoffing children, the sin of David, the golden calf and the rest. I re-

[1] January, 1930.

membered the uncomfortable mornings when I had sat before a poor, limited woman who had tried to impress upon us the dire morals of these stories.

Beside the quarterlies were booklets making an appeal for funds to aid superannuated country clergymen. These contained pictures of circuit riders, saddles and saddle-bags, and many portraits of bearded old gentlemen. Their devoted service in behalf of their flocks was recited. These had labored in God's vineyard, and should not now be left in want. They had been soldiers of the Lord, carrying His crusade.

Had they been? I stopped and asked myself. What had their fifty years of circuit riding accomplished? They had seen the lands further impoverished, the roads more rutted, families moving to town and city, education only slightly bettered. How had their patience and exertion told in a fuller life for the average person in that community, for greater comfort and security?

I concluded that I could give them something for pity's sake, but not on the score of progress.

The whole environment of my childhood came back to me. Two themes ran through it—poverty and evangelical religion. The first was the occasion of the second. We were still in the backwash of the destruction wrought by the Civil War. Life was a struggle for most families of our acquaintance. The one little rich boy stands out in my memory as an anomaly. Being lean of goods, people were anguished spiritually. Their economic want was sublimated, so far as they were able, into religious emotionalism. They cried out to God continually, and in this tried to find comfort. They went a step further. Economic sufficiency being unattainable, it was declared superfluous or even wicked. A harsh and unlovely asceticism developed. Sympathies were narrow, thoughts intolerant. The veriest infant was made acquainted with the lapses of the ancient Jews, and all God's wrath at their behavior was thundered in his ears.

A sweet atmosphere in which to grow up! Though I look back upon it with a shudder, I hope I have learned tolerance. I know that this was a phase in the social history of the South, only one of the miserable consequences of war and a mistaken economic scheme of things. The revival meetings, which with dreadful drama sought to pull children down into the sorrows of their elders, were a result of cotton and slavery, secession and surrender.

The old country neighborhood of which I first spoke is a backwater eddy, but in the South as a whole that day of poverty and piety is passing, or has passed. What is the lesson of it for those of us who tasted its physical bitterness and spiritual pathology, and yet find ourselves vigorous in the new era of growing plenty and freed minds?

The lesson is, for the South at least, and I suspect more widely, that the possibility of good arrived with advances in production and in fortunate economic contrivance, and never sprang from prayers flung up to God. The new deities are those of the Machine and Science, and very rightly, for they have given us more than scripture could.

Here were the Poor Whites. I need not recount their story. It was one of neglect, banishment, ignorance, poverty—almost descent to the condition of aborigines. With great doses of religion, they sank deeper into hopelessness. Came the cotton factory, which opened to them the door to cash earnings, neighborly contacts, a measure of self-respect. There have been plans for their betterment, some of them founded on religious motives, but all of these have waited upon material advance. The Poor Whites in the cotton mills have had to pass through deep waters, but I believe they are now emerging, and again it is through economic forces and not through obedience to injunctions to love God and be good. They are forming unions to secure shorter hours and higher wages, and these things spell righteousness.

Well disposed people prayed for the amelioration of the fate of the Negro and formed societies to forward his education and fair treatment. But his liberation from chattel slavery came as the result of economic forces, and in the long years between the Civil War and the World War he virtually marked time until a new turn of events, not looked for, befell him. Restriction upon immigration and resulting demand for Negro workers to make steel and build automobiles have done more for the Negro than three centuries of Christian prayer. First of all, in huge numbers, he has moved away from his old vassalage on the land; he gets a job and a chance of a better job; he gets a good school and a degree of social recognition. There have been mishaps in the advance, of course, and will be many more, but looking at the American Negro from Gold Coast to Detroit, his notable aptitude for religion has brought him nothing, and work opportunities have brought him all he has.

I remember so well plans for making country life more pleasant. There were to be more schools, and these were to be centers of community activity. Roads were to be improved. The farm wife, it was alleged on good authority, cooked the family's food laved in fat, and this was to be remedied by home economics experts who would go from house to house with a new gospel of spinach and broiling. Isolation was to be overcome by clubs, fostered by main force. But little was accomplished.

Then, behold! The Ford automobile! Salvation in a new aspect! Its differential was high enough to clear the ruts, its strong little heart refused to stop beating, its sinewy frame withstood wrenches and shocks, it thrived on neglect. It was cheap, and it became universal. It improved the roads under its wheels, increased the value of lands which it brought closer to markets, consolidated the schools which had remained divorced despite all pleadings, and gave the backwoods farmer a town and a thousand new neighbors. It brought him cash for perishable farm products, freedom from the old slavery to landlord credit, it put him in motion and invited him to " step on it."

Religious education in the South is different from what it used to be, and religion as a whole is tremendously diluted, Tennessee notwithstanding. The church used to be the whole voice of society, but now it finds its functions divided around between many social agencies—the factory, the school, the market and the club.

It is fortunate that this is so. It makes for less anguish and more enjoyment. It does not make for wickedness, whatever that means. Prosperity is a blessing, not a curse. Only disappointed reactionaries can damn it, though of these there appear to be enough. If the church survives, in the South and elsewhere in America, it must be by clearing away the old frown and replacing it by a smile, and by recognizing that the love of God really means friendliness to the expanding world about us.

24. Analyzing Ourselves in the South [1]

The South of the last fifty years has been lacking in critical faculty. This has been due to two main causes: first, the weight of a static tradition, and second, preoccupation of active minds in the work of creation. The matter may be examined under four heads: religious, cultural, political, and economic.

[1] 1929.

1. Our religious and spiritual life. Here the past has stretched out its hand and held us fast. We have remained dogmatic, evangelical. The church has turned in a squirrel-wheel—noisy, getting nowhere. The church has offered no interpretation of changing social life. We have remained like Mary enraptured at the Master's feet, and have refused to have a part in the workaday world, or be like Martha "anxious about many things." The church, with a tremendous grasp on Southern life, has failed to take the easy chance of leadership which has been presented to it. It has not utilized the best approach, the most natural approach which the South has—the religious—to racial amity and industrial justice. The most spectacular proof of this is the recent championing of fundamentalism.

2. Our cultural life. Here we have shown more hopeful signs than in our religious life. Consider drama, fiction, sculpture, scholarship, perhaps education. In these fields, in the main, we have been concerned about two things—(a) reaching a degree of technical proficiency, and (b) the picturing of local types. In the first particular we have made progress. As to the second, we have principally perpetuated the memory of the Old South of romance, whether in the stories of Page and Cable or the monuments to Confederate heroes. Now begins a new literature, mostly fiction, which makes a step in advance by essaying a realistic defining of certain groups, such as the Negro, the mountaineer, the tenant farmer.

Here is an element of self-analysis, but the subject-matter is what has existed for a long time. Literature is slow in its recognitions. There are few novels, stories or plays dealing with the industrial life of the South, the conflict between field and factory, or the new social world being created under our eyes. Reviews in the South, where they exist, are apt to be "literary" rather than critical of social conditions.

3. Our political life. Dissent from domination of the one party has been growing, but sub rosa. It has been local and, except as a straw in the stream, unimportant. Generally there has been political stagnation, with the only discussion turning not upon issues, but upon personal quarrels of contending candidates. In the presidential campaign of 1928 the South swallowed, perhaps with some enthusiasm, a platform which admits the wisdom of protection. It is too early to know in how far this represents conviction stimulated by economic interest, and in how far acceptance of the tariff has been dictated by national political exigency. If it be lasting, it is extremely significant.

4. Our economic and industrial life. Here change has been most rapid so far as physical accomplishment is concerned. Agriculture, naturally enough, has shown fewer alterations than industry, but perhaps because diversification of crops and expertness in farming method have required deliberate social propaganda, the quality of self-analysis has been

ahead of any self-criticism that has appeared in the realm of manufacturing and its concomitants.

In the latter, private initiative has been sufficient to sweep the process of exploitation ahead. The race has been so rapid and spectacular that the public has sat in the bleachers and shouted for the winner in each heat. The more articulate in the community have profited by the Industrial Revolution, and hence have been silent as to its ill effects. The underpaid worker has had no voice of his own. The Southern textile operative has had little assistance from his fellows in the North because these have been engaged in a desperate attempt to preserve their own industrial status against the killing competition of the South. Nor has the Southern industrial worker found the college community alert or vocal in the face of economic happenings. In the field of changes in social relationship we are distinguished by unawareness and lack of curiosity, let alone purpose.

If these things are substantially true, then an early need of the South is self-realization—in its own posture at home and in the eye of the nation. In assistance to this end the church offers nothing. Literature and the cultural arts move slowly, finding their material in social phenomena only after these have become fairly fixed. Politics will be merely a function of the dominant economic interest; to look for courage or pioneering in the run of political spokesmen would be to put the cart before the horse. Industry itself is not promising in the particular of social analysis. Capitalists are not ruminative themselves nor anxious to listen to others. They have an aspect of tenderness sometimes (welfare work), but this is often the scabbard and holds a blade. Competition among industrialists and growing scarcity of workers will after a time bring better standards in industry and forced recognition of such a necessary device as unionism. But these developments, while certain in their efficacy, will be slow in coming.

For the present we have to look to Southern colleges, universities, and enlightened newspaper men. Southern newspapers on the whole have preserved a tradition of disinterested advocacy superior to that of the press in the sections where industry and commerce have been longer established. As the South becomes richer, institutions of higher learning can afford to give effort not only to teaching, but to inquiry. Much can be done immediately, with the good effect of preparing the public mind for further social changes which are sure to come.

25. SLIPPERS AND OLD SORREL [1]

Is there such a thing as a cheerful basement? Dampness strikes through the walls and spreads gloom. Low ceilings oppress. Perhaps that front kitchen in Carlyle's house in Cheyne Row is an exception. After wandering through the bleak chambers and bleaker improvisation of a study above, you expand to the coziness of its grate fire and its

[1] June, 1929.

torpid gray cat which has not only looked at a king but shaken hands with him. Through small high windows you can see feet go tripping or trudging past, but you are content to watch the flame dance on bright pans or strike a glow from selfrespecting iron pots.

Not to descend to very dungeons or catacombs, I suppose the underground rooms in Manchester which served to pen the factory operatives a hundred years ago vie with the dankest. They recall the stout young Engels' imprecations of 1844, and the devoted ministrations of Richard Oastler during an earlier seizure of the mill fever.

I encountered a basement recently which stands forward in the list of the world's pensive and depressing places. It is in the bottom of the chapel of the old Southern college to which Robert E. Lee went as president after his surrender at Appomattox. Here have been put relics of the great leader of the Confederacy, with some mementoes of his lieutenant, Stonewall Jackson.

They comprise a somber company. The yellow sash in which Lee met Grant in the farmhouse, and the silver spurs, now dull with tarnish. The drinking cup, the clock, the cutlery that were always in his tent on the field. Faded specimens of his handwriting, locks of his hair, the pair of bedroom slippers which he wore at the last. There is a photograph, too, of Jackson's war horse, taken at a great age. Old Sorrel's knees are bent piteously forward, his head is no longer erect. It was too bad to make such a picture, and better to remember only the fatal ride through the woods of Chancellorsville.

A troop of tourists from New Jersey came in while I went from one glass case to another. I was inclined to reproach myself that they felt more tenderness for these souvenirs of the Old South than did I, a native son. My father is a Mississippian, my mother a South Carolinian. I wondered whether I of the younger generation was not a profanation to this sacred place. I edged away from the custodian, kindly eager to show and explain. Perhaps, in respect to a long tradition, I should have been content, after dropping my silver in the box, to go away and hold my peace.

We are nearly seventy years away from the surrender of the Old South. Our Confederate veterans' homes still contain a few gray-clad figures. I hope they find sunny places on the long wooden galleries. In the main those whose feelings would be hurt by utter frankness in one of their own blood are gone. For those Sons of Confederate Veterans who have taken up the old cry in a false note I have no respect.

Slippers and Old Sorrel. What do they connote to the South of today? Mostly, of course, the antebellum leaders got us into trouble. One is not so much inclined to shed a tear for them that they were the knights of the "Lost Cause" as that they were the knaves of a lost South. They took the easiest way with their economic environment, and were fertile in rationalizations of their course. They pursued a wasteful, staple agriculture; only a few paid more than lip service to the utility of manufactures, while most of them treated industry with fear or contempt. They developed the elaborate story of States' rights (to know how elaborate one must read Calhoun's " Disquisition on Government ") to cover the tracks of slavery. They grew into a personally pleasing aristocracy, allowing the Poor Whites to be shouldered aside into penury and ignorance.

Their vaunted chivalry was thus a mockery. They served their own interests. They rested their economic system upon the back of the chattel slave, leaving their unpropertied white brothers without even the measure of paternalism meted out to useful dependents. They were supposed to be not only free from the burgeois vices of the North but exceedingly genteel. But their culture, if we leave aside their soft voices, was a myth. They had no music, no art but Georgian porticoes and beaten biscuit, and a scanty few men of letters. They had no inventiveness, for their whole life was stagnation. Their men of science were almost accidental, for learning was metaphysical and was applied in oratory. One may assert they made a fine art of politics, but they possessed no truly representative institutions.

They had no gift for communal living or enterprise. William Gregg, a South Carolina manufacturer who found himself lonely in a plantation environment, declared that the basis of improvement must be a good home for the average man and concern for the welfare of neighbors. But Jefferson had given them, as F. S. Oliver has said, the ideal of the bee rather than of the hive. They showed small talent for reading the signs of their own times. They inhibited themselves from the national adventure.

A fair test of greatness in a group of leaders is the ability of their system to live and develop after them. But these men of the Old South marked the end of an era. They never properly dug in, nor invested anything for the future. Their maxim, toward land, capital, and labor, and toward their political reasoning as well, was exploitation. It may be said of them, in the final fling of civil war, as Hamilton said of other fanatics: "The love-sick partisans of that country appear to regard her as the epitome of the universe; to have adopted for their motto, 'All for love, and the world well lost.'"

It would not have been so bad, even so, had they left the South simply exhausted after the conflict. But they left her without recuperative power in the old habit. In a one-crop agriculture, which had banished ingenuity, there was no trick of recovery. Wounds gaped wider and became gangrenous during Reconstruction. In the decade since the World War we have witnessed Germany, depleted in man power, shorn of colonies, circumscribed and scorned by the nations and loaded with debt by her victors, scrambling to her feet with the assistance of industry, and where industry was shackled, coming back by the bare knowledge of industry. But in the South the economic system had lent itself to destruction, the stamping out of the last spark. The plantation plug had pulled his last share through the shallow furrow; no action resulted from thrashing a dead horse.

The Old South expired like a fine gentleman who, after protracted years as a burden to his family, has passed on, leaving sons and daughters penniless. What do we owe to the memory of this gallant? He once had a grand manner, but even in his heyday his linen was habitually soiled. Why embalm his remains and keep his few belongings like relics at the shrine of a saint? We paid him too much honor while he lived, and furthermore sad reminders of his handiwork are all about us in the South this long time afterward—poverty, race hatred, sterile fields, the childish and violent crowd gulled by the demagogue.[2]

The South after the Civil War had to begin again, with no inheritance from human contrivance. There was scarcely so much as a single idea which could be salvaged for the new departure. It is indicative of the prostration of the Old South that its few projects which held the seed of hope had been neglected and were not encouraged to multiply. The Graniteville cotton factory in South Carolina and the Oxmoor furnace in Tennessee were antecedent to the postwar development in time, but hardly in influence.

The New South of industry and commerce, compared to the Old South of cotton, tobacco, rice and

---

[2] Several critics have mistakenly supposed that this paragraph refers to General Lee. On the contrary, it means to personalize the Old South.

sugar, is a steel blade compared to a stone shard. The South produces now more than eight billion dollars in manufactured goods. Not only Americans, but Europeans as well, look upon it as a promising field for industrial enterprise and move their factories to its cheap labor and hydro-electric power. It is experiencing an industrial revolution huge and swift. Through this development the South is offered a progressive future.

But even in the midst of the new prosperity the old tradition pursues us calamitously. The Poor White, formerly expelled by slavery, has the door of opportunity opened to him only if he endures his own servitude of long hours and low wages in the cotton factories. His employer, accustomed enough to paternalism, translates the old habit into graceful patronage in company-owned mill villages, only to show every unfairness when the workers demand an approach to justice. There is no chivalry in starving striking operatives into submission.

The public mind which used to be led by the articulate plantation aristocrats and their dependents is now dancing to the tune of a new dominant class—this time the capitalist. Eventually, through the mere instrument of industrial maturity, we shall reach national standards of labor legislation, political participation and literacy, and by then it will be clearly known that the South of romance, long ago or since, was just a literary hoax, good only for a mammy song.

26. Sand-Hillers North and South[1]

Was it Harriet Martineau, or perhaps Captain Hall, who drew such a distinction between the economic virtues of the inhabitants of Cape Cod and those of the sand hills of the South? Whoever the first critic was, the comparison has often been made since, and always to the disparagement of the Carolinians and Georgians. The Cape Codders have been called thrifty, hardy, active, industrious, while the "Red Necks," "Crackers," "Dirt Eaters," and Poor Whites generally, have come down in history as lazy and improvident. It has often been said that the Southerners are even degenerate.

There is now good reason to question the general impression.

There are several points of fundamental similarity between these particular groups of Northerners and Southerners. Both inhabit sandy districts yielding little to tillage. Both are of English stock (with a mixture of Scotch-Irish among the Southerners), and descendants of original settlers. Both were for generations producers of a single staple, and both in recent years have shifted to new occupations.

New England has enjoyed too much of a monopoly in the making of American literature, and surely in the writing of American history, for us not to know of life on Cape Cod. Provincetown and Plymouth commenced the saga. The light, stony, and altogether unresponsive soil drawing men to the water,

[1] September, 1926.

they became great fishermen and merchant sailors. Every indentation in the coast was a harbor for a native fleet. Nets were dried on every sand spit. Harpoons stood about in corners as familiarly as walking canes. To take an illustration a little off the mainland, half the houses in Nantucket had "widow's walks" on their roofs, from which anxious wives could scan the sea. Those left at home on diminutive farms scratched unremittingly about the rocks.

The picture of the sand-hiller in the South has been quite different. Not having enough money to purchase slaves, he was pushed into the economic and social background. Cotton culture with Negro labor took from the Poor White such employment as he had previously had in manufacturing. Iron furnaces and fulling-mills were abandoned in favor of planting on a large scale. The sand-hiller became a tenant of the slave owner, chronically in debt, and raised a large family of children, who, without education or incentive, repeated the father's fate, and their children after them. Some were mere squatters, growing patches of cotton on sufferance. Lean, sallow, tobacco-chewing, whisky-drinking, distrusting the upper Whites, hating the Negroes and by the Negroes despised, these people were patterns of the mean and sordid.

But how is the situation today? In many respects it is reversed.

It is the Cape Codder who is now seen in degeneration—economic and social rather than physical, to be sure, but still very striking. The glory of the whaling days is gone. Nearby, at New Bedford, the oldest of the whaling ships is carefully preserved, held in a huge box of sand. She has survived to see her sisters swept from the ocean, or ignominiously converted into barges. Beside the ship is a bronze tablet listing the thirty-two owners who gave her for an exhibit. It reads like a death-roll of departed enterprise. " Whaling Enshrined," indeed! The old free roving over the seven seas had nothing in common with this painted ship upon a painted ocean. The rolling old seaman who meets you at the gang plank and explains every detail of the vessel's equipment, once made voyages in her, and now has the heart to act as showman on her so steady deck.

The rest of the fishing has gone to the Pacific Coast, or Alaska, or been taken over by big companies in the East. The Cape even imports lobsters from Nova Scotia waters. Old fellows who a generation ago raced their ships into port, and are still scrupulously called " captain," are glad to pick up a few quarters by rowing summer tourists about familiar harbors.

The entertainment of the tourist and the summer guest has become the great industry. Men who could build boats now whittle out toy windmills for sale along the roads. Pieces of Sandwich glass are sold at high prices, while the factory has fallen into decay. Every wide place on the highway has its tea house ("The Lobster Claw," of all the names I have noticed, is most accurately descriptive of their practices). The houses of the Winthrops now are blazoned with "The Purple Parrot" and "The Blue Smock." The very graves of their ancestors are made light of by this commercial generation, which sells decipherings of "all the funny epitaphs."

A decade of golf has sufficed for the digging up of more rocks from the fields than was accomplished by thirty decades of Cape Cod farming. The winter population of the towns is made up in no small part of those who, in summer, find employment in mowing greens and fairways. The Cape Codders—old Americans, vigorous and adventurous—are now lackeys and panderers to July and August guests, and the rest of the long year look forward to a return of the spending horde. They endure with composure the visible signs of the insult, for they are well paid. But an outsider may resent the affront to ancient prowess. If here and there—in Barnstable, Yarmouth, Falmouth—a sea captain potters about his retired cottage, the streets are full of Brockton shoe manufacturers and wholesale cracker salesmen from Boston wearing white caps marked "Commodore."

And what is the case of the sand-hillers in the South? If it may be said of the Cape Codders, with Rose of Washington Square, that they have no future, but, oh, what a past! the Carolinas tell a different story. There the past was dreary, but tomorrow promises much more. Poor Whites, not much enriched by " rural life " programs and home dietetic lessons, are entering the cotton mills by thousands, there to find cash wages, social intercourse, schools, and amusements. Native operatives are rising to be foremen and superintendents. Cotton mill employment is being greatly increased by the number of New England companies which are moving plants to the South. New industries are springing up, and these all help the towns and the farms. Many a " neck of the woods " in North Carolina which a few years ago could show only a grass-grown track in the sand, is now cut through with the finest concrete road that money and engineering can construct. Almost every hill has a new house, not a few of them solid school houses.

Recently the growing of peaches has opened an unexpected source of prosperity, particularly in North Carolina. Old fields abandoned to broomsedge and " blackjacks," and which within five or six years sold for $8 an acre, are now yielding the finest crops of fruit. Once inconsequential way-stations now have sidings for busy packing sheds and shipping platforms. Owners of a few acres, never before suspected of enterprise, are following the lead of large orchardists. They are discovering, besides, that sand which, even heavily dosed with " sody," would grow cotton only a foot high, will yield watermelons two feet long.

It will be years yet before the Southern sand-hiller gains his full economic independence. But he is on the path to a new day, while Cape Cod lives to lament the passing of the old.

27. Social Education

Everybody knows that the South is making spectacular progress in public education, particularly in the development of primary and secondary schools. The colleges and universities are increasing their enrollments, and the position of the State institutions of higher learning is becoming stronger.

The preparatory schools, being new growth, are more up-to-date in educational methods than the colleges, and it is these high schools in town and country—well equipped, well taught, well administered, well *conceived* withal—which are to mould the public opinion of the generation just coming on the scene.

It is important that they should give socialized training. No section of the country needs it so much as the South. Nowhere else are problems of industry, agriculture and race so complicated and so pressing. Other parts of America have their difficulties, but in these the issues are better understood than is the case in the South. Manufactures in New England and the Middle Atlantic States raise questions of trade unions and the tariff; ship subsidies wait upon political adherence rather than more theoretical argumentation; the farmers of the wheat belt have their distresses, but a program of remedies is sufficiently bruited; timber conservation and irrigation are technical matters, and coal mining approaches the day of deliberate social engineering.

But in the South both economic facts and public reaction to these facts are ill understood. The South, in a brief space of time, has experienced tremendous and sudden economic changes. It had an agricultural system as primitive as India's, with a peasantry as backward as Russia's. It had a slavery so deeply intrenched that it killed inventiveness, destroyed diversification, impoverished literature, perverted politics, and precluded art. It had civil war, which reversed old ambitions, rendered the currency comic, made the public credit a laughing stock, and fundamentally altered the labor system at one fell swoop. Followed then Reconstruction, with humiliation, looting and vengeance the dominant characteristics of a general turmoil. Next arrived, nearly overnight, an Industrial Revolution as swift and vigorous as that in England, with not long afterwards changes in farming methods and a far-flung educational crusade.

These kaleidoscopic happenings, falling pell mell one upon another, have been bewildering. The South has not known how other societies have met these developments. Attacks and defenses have not had familiar lines in which to range themselves. Problems which with more experienced peoples have resolved themselves into questions of profit and loss, economic advantage and defeat, and trials of strength between well marshalled forces, have tried our souls in the South as a whole people. We have always had a certain talent for conceiving perplexities as public matters. The old aristocracy, while highly opinionated and efficient in its determinations, thought of itself as spokesman for a dumb multitude. We have invested public discussion of affairs with an inflated mysticism.

Our long domination by a dogmatic clergy and a religion which had precious few connections with the realities of social life has borne great part in this. The facts of our possessing only one political party and one assertive economic group (the white people pushing the black into the background) have not helped to define issues. Charles Lamb might have said of the Southerner as he did of the beloved Joseph Munden, that " his pots and his ladles are as grand and as primal as the seething-pots and hooks seen in old prophetic vision. A tub of butter, contemplated by him, amounts to a Platonic idea. . . . He stands wondering, amid the commonplace materials of life, like primæval man with the sun and stars above him."

Our inheritance from slavery has proved a great disability here. The work of the South was done by blacks who did not talk nor think, and who acted only in accordance with an unchanging routine. The slave owners who had mind and voice had very little intimate contact with economic activities as such. Overseers stood between them and the plantation forces. Of manufactures only a tiny minority knew anything. Banking was badly bungled. Railroad building was successful so far as great construction was concerned, but financing was by governmental subsidy rather than private subscription, and the ambition to run lines linking seacoast ports with the West and Southwest lessened direct connections with the North that would have been wholesome.

Ante-bellum stirrings toward economic progress were motivated largely by the project of political separatism. The commercial conventions held in the South from 1837 to the outbreak of the Civil War exhibited an inevitable degeneration of economic planning in the direction of political infatuation. The merchants, sincerer than other delegates, were swamped by oratory. The respectable desire for direct trade with Europe gave way before the demand for reopening of the slave trade. In a later day a man like Governor Hammond, of South Carolina, might have been a constructive leader. As it was he took a scientific interest in agricultural method and made a speech or two as a sop thrown to the advocates of home manufacturing, but mainly he gave himself over to Nullification, militia parades, and a strident and crazy confidence in Southern superiority on all points.

Our middle class developed late and slowly. With its rise has come an economic progress better than all the debates and State papers. Small farms, sound banks, thriving commercial undertakings, and mighty cotton mills have speeded up the process of social evolution. These are transferring our occupations from the realm of conjecture to that of activity. The desire for private profit has been more wholesome than that of public applause. The movement toward material wellbeing has brought its temporary and great calamities—the impoverished tenant whites, Negroes restless on the threshhold of industrial entrance, company-owned villages of cotton mill operatives limited in self-determination. But these are in course of solution, simply because we have now what we never had before—the moving force of economic enterprise for the sake of enterprise. Development is on all lines and for every private purpose, and does not show, as once, the " digging in " of one interest, which sought to draw to itself every public sanction.

It is becoming slowly apparent in the South that the building of economic strength waits upon diversification of pursuits. It is being seen that the Old South, devoting exclusive attention to one activity (cotton cultivation) and thus seeking economic preeminence and independence, was erecting a fool's paradise. The event proved that the boasted independence was really an abject dependence, and the lesson sinks in.

The eccentric mirrors which by indirect reflections pictured the South to itself are being discredited. We are commencing to see face to face. Education in the South ought to take its cue from these latter-day economic happenings. The confusion of vision that persists in regard to our internal social problems can be cleared up much more rapidly, of course, if the schools are actively aware of economic occurrence and help to cultivate an economic point of view.

Books on "civics," with their inconsequential fol-de-rol, ought to be replaced by texts setting forth in simple terms the economic history of the South, and presenting such matters as farm incomes, school consolidation, good roads, race relations, labor unionism. The realities of economic democracy are of far more importance to us now than the fictions of political democracy. The presentation to the school child of the immaculate machinery of legislative elections is in sharp contrast, if anyone stops to think about it, to the sorry personnel and uninformed discussions which actually are found in our capitols. But the achievements of business enterprise in the South are far in advance of our recognition of them, and the issues which they raise need definition.

The Southern child is being born into a local industrial, agricultural and intellectual revolution, to say nothing of the national and international surprises that impend. How can the child find himself or how can the society which he is to make be a rational one, unless we turn attention to the queries of economic life? Prizes offered in the schools by the Daughters of the Confederacy for essays on such topics as Civil War Prisons ought to be left to older historical ghouls. It is criminal to put children at such exhumations, while they can look about them at tall green stalks of corn, fat hogs that loll where the " razorback " sprinted, electric transmission towers, and smoking chimneystacks. And these material things call for the exercise of all the sweet humanism which the Old South has to contribute.